AF412798

The Secrets of Successful Options Trading

Neil Osborne

THE INDEX OPTION

The Secrets of Successful Options Trading

Neil Osborne

Rushmere Wynne
England

First published 1996
This edition (2nd impression) 1997

British Library Cataloguing in Publication Data.
A catalogue record for this book is available from the British Library.

ISBN 0 948035 24 2

Designed by:
MacWing

Published by:
Rushmere Wynne Limited
4-5 Harmill, Grovebury Road,
Leighton Buzzard, Bedfordshire LU7 8FF

Printed by:
Bookcraft Book Printers & Binders,
First Avenue, Westfield Trading Estate,
Midsomer Norton, Bath, Avon BA3 4BS

Wealth Warning

While all reasonable care has been taken to ensure that the details in this book are true and not misleading at the time of publication, no liability is accepted by Rushmere Wynne, Neil Osborne or their servants or agents, for the use of information contained herein in any circumstances connected with actual trading or otherwise. Neither Rushmere Wynne nor Neil Osborne nor their servants or agents are responsible for any errors or omissions within this book. It is published for information purposes only and shall not constitute investment advice. All descriptions, examples and calculations contained in this book are for guidance purposes only and should not be treated as definitive.

Certain investments or investment services mentioned in this book may not be suitable for all readers and further advice should be sought from your Investment Adviser in this respect. Please note that the value of investments and the income derived from them may fall as well as rise and you may get back less than originally invested. Past performance is not necessarily a guide to future performance.

Contents

Introduction

IMAGINE you are visiting a large city such as London for the first time. Eight million people, thousands of roads, streets, lanes and alleys with the odd circus or two thrown in to confuse the foreign tourist. There appears to be no rhyme or reason to the layout of the streets, like the great cities of America, or even a planned centre such as Paris.

But very quickly you start to find your way round.

Buckingham Palace, you realise is joined to Trafalgar Square by The Mall. The No.15 bus will take you from the shops at Oxford Circus to the Tower of London. The Tube map pays little attention to what is above ground and yet thousands of passengers every day arrive at their destinations with the minimum of fuss, making the map one of the triumphs of modern cartography.

Now transfer these thoughts to the traded options market.

It's a labyrinth, too. And the sign-posts look as odd as some in the capital: Naked Writing sounds like an indelicate art, especially if you are involved at the same time in a Vertical Bear Call Spread. And what about the Long Straddle strategy - perhaps the investor should be in the Long Strangle strategy instead?

And didn't your friends and colleagues warn you about options investments and how you could lose everything in a matter of seconds, including the shirt off your own back? And what about the pin-striped sharks who'd eat you, the investor, before you could utter the words "strike price"?

But then didn't your mother warn you about wicked London? And girls who go into pubs by themselves? Only after one thing, eh? And watch out for those smogs and don't stand on the cracks in the pavement, dear!

Forget about not understanding calculus to work out the mathematics of chance - there's enough computer hardware and software to answer every query a million times over (and that's why we have provided you with a free Options Evaluator disk to show you how user-friendly the system can be).

Use this book like an A-Z of London. Concentrate on how to get from A to B safely and forget about the highly complex world around you. Certainly admire the scenery and explore a side-street here and there but don't expose yourself to the proverbial mugger or leave your wallet sticking out of your back pocket to tempt the pickpocket.

Stay within the parameters of the book until you are sure of your expertise and your judgement. And always follow the strategies where you can lose no more than your original stake.

Definitions

An index option is

A flexible financial instrument that derives its value from the level of an 'underlying' index, eg. FT-SE 100, S&P 500 etc. Index options can be used to 'hedge' or protect a portfolio against a fall in the market or implemented in speculative strategies.

And some more key definitions . . .

Call option

An option that confers upon the owner the right to buy the underlying at a predetermined price (the exercise price) at some point in the future.

Derivative

A financial asset whose value is derived from the value of another underlying instrument.

Exercise

This term refers to when an option holder exercises his/her option.

Finite Risk Strategy

An option strategy in which the maximum loss is quantifiable and known from the onset of the position – examples include buying options, and certain 'spread' strategies – see section on Option Strategies.

Put Option

An option that confers upon the owner the right to sell the underlying shares at a predetermined price (the exercise price) at some point in the future.

The full glossary of option terminology can be found on pages 163-166

Chapter 1
UNDERSTANDING THE
BASICS OF INDEX OPTIONS

Welcome to the new and exciting world of index options! The purpose of this book is twofold; firstly, to demystify traded options (specifically index options) by providing a gentle introduction to the subject in a clear, jargon-free manner and, secondly, to present you with some profitable, finite risk index option strategies and techniques. Furthermore, you will discover under what conditions these strategies are most likely to be successful (ie. profitable).

Ideally, you will have had some experience with equities (shares), though no prior knowledge of options is assumed. The book therefore begins with an explanation of the general concept of an option, types of option and an introduction to some of the more common terminology associated with options.

For the benefit of readers completely new to options, we will discuss briefly equity options (ie. options on shares) in this chapter. Thereafter, the focus moves on to index options (we will cover, in particular, the FT-SE 100 index option). The main point to grasp is the concept of an option. Thereafter, the knowledge gained can be applied to various categories of options, eg. share options, index options, gilt options etc. If you are already familiar with options it will do you no harm to read this chapter. However, you may may decide to move on to the next chapter.

Options offer an exciting, flexible and fun way to achieve investment objectives. For far too long, the UK private investor has ignored this interesting and rewarding investment medium. I have heard several private investors claim adamantly: "I do fine just investing in shares – I don't want to get involved in those new fangled option things!" – before realising that they were missing out on all sorts of profit-making opportunities (and quickly changing their minds!).

Hopefully, this book will help you to unravel the mysteries (and occasional gems) of traded options. This book is targeted primarily at the many thousands of private investors who have had some experience of shares and may (or may not) have considered options as an alternative form of investment (or as a complement to their current investments) but remain wary or sceptical of options.

The rational investor

Before taking a close look at options, let us take a closer look at why people invest, and what is offered by the various investment choices (ie. shares, bonds, commodities etc.) available to the private investor. Without getting too technical and talking about risk aversion and indifference curves, there is one single and simple motivating force behind all investments made – and that is profit. In other words **a rational investor undertakes an investment in order to make a profit.**

The more opportunities there are to invest the more likely you as an investor are to achieve your goal of profitability. Therefore, the more flexible (in terms of investments offered) that an investment (stock, gilt, option, future etc.) is, the more opportunities there will be for you as an investor to make money. It really is that simple.

Let me explain further. People generally invest in the shares of a company because they believe that the value of the shares they have bought will increase over a period of time, thus allowing them to realise a profit when the shares are sold at a later date. In gambling parlance, therefore, the investor is 'betting' on the value of the share purchased increasing. But investing in shares is 'one sided' because, as an investor, you can only make money when the value of the company you have backed is increasing and you will lose money if the value of the concern decreases. If an investor thinks that the share price of a particular company is going to fall, he/she cannot (and generally must not) invest in the shares of the company.

As an investor in options, the investment landscape is not so 'one sided' – ie. there are profit making strategies (opportunities to make a profit) available to you if the share price rises, falls, or remains unchanged. Additionally, as a result of gearing (which I'll explain later), a move in the 'right' direction that might have resulted in a 10% profit for an investor in shares could easily turn to be a 100% (or more) profit for an investor in options. So having now stirred up a burning desire in you to know more about these wonderful, flexible investment instruments, let us take our first step in the understanding of trading options.

The basic concept

The idea of an option is remarkably simple: possibly many people apply this concept several times a day without even being aware of doing so. For various reasons (largely due to a misunderstanding) several myths have arisen surrounding options. Originally a risk management tool, options have now become the 'bogey men' of the UK private investor community, with many being put off by the unfamiliar terms and complex option pricing equations wielded by 'the professionals'. You'll be glad to hear that a large proportion of all the jargon and complex formulae is really irrelevant to the private investor. A large number of private clients hold the view that the world of options exists in a rarefied atmosphere only for the financially sophisticated or mathematical geniuses and not for the lay person. The result is that many private investors are missing out on many of what could be profitable investment opportunities. In the US, private investor use of options accounts for a significant number of trades conducted on the Chicago Board of Options Exchange and a similar relatively high proportion of option trades (by UK standards) are conducted by private investors in Amsterdam.

Let's take a closer look at options to find out exactly what they are. Options are financial instruments (investments, if you like), that are 'based' on various things like shares, bonds or an index (eg. the FT-SE 100 index). The 'thing' on which an option is 'based' is known as the **underlying**. When I say an option is 'based' on an underlying, what that means is that changes in the price of the underlying will cause the price of the option to change as well.

Don't worry if you don't understand this yet, as I'll provide several examples and analogies later in this chapter so that by the time you come to the end, you should be quite familiar with what an option is (and a lot more besides). Like all disciplines, options have their own terminology which tends to intimidate and confuse the beginner – but once the basic terms and concepts have been learnt and understood, it all becomes unbelievably easy.

So what is so special about options anyway? The beauty of an option is the **flexibility** it offers you as an investor. For almost every view that an investor may have on the underlying, there is an almost infinite array of option strategies that may be employed. This subtle statement conceals a very potent truth – for **every** possible movement in the underlying, there exists a profitable option position that can be implemented. In case you haven't yet realised the significance of this statement, I will repeat it by saying that what this means is that index options provide you with the opportunity to turn **every** possible movement (or lack thereof) of the market into **cash in the bank**. The reality is that with index options you, as an index option investor, are given the **opportunity to make money regardless of whether the market is moving up, down, or not even moving at all!** Investors (particularly private individuals) have never had it so good. This sort of flexibility is not available to investors in 'traditional' investment instruments such as shares, bonds, commodities etc.

Private investors have been generally left out of partaking in this interesting, flexible and fun way of turning movements in the markets into money in the bank largely as a result of their own fears. "So where is the catch?" I hear you ask. The catch (for there is indeed one) is that you have to be able to spot the strategy most likely to be profitable from the several that are often 'seemingly appropriate' given an investment scenario. This is not quite as onerous a task as it may seem at first, as there will be specific examples later on in this book which will show you how you can help 'tilt the odds' in your favour.

Up to now, only a relatively few UK private investors have enjoyed this 'secret' and have been actively engaged in the index options market. However, there is one benefit of this lack of participation by UK private investors in the option markets (you may well have guessed): as so few private investors use options in general, they are under researched and not exploited to the maximum benefit. It is therefore possible for the astute investor who spends a little time and effort in understanding options, to obtain an 'edge' and consequently produce far superior returns. With the help of this book, all will be revealed and you too will learn of strategies to make money when the market is going up, down, or looks likely to remain relatively unchanged. With a bit of careful foresight and luck, you can turn movements in the market into cash in your account.

There has been a lot of scaremongering and many misconceptions surrounding options (this is largely due to ignorance) and it is my intention in this book to dispel these myths. The two most popular misconceptions about options are:

Myth No 1   *Options are incredibly difficult to understand.*

Fact   The concept of an option is really quite simple as we shall see. Options have existed in one form or another for almost as long as man has been conducting commerce and trade.

Myth No 2   *Options are extremely risky. If you trade in options you can be 'wiped out' completely in a matter of seconds – and end up owing a fortune.*

Fact   All investments are risky, and although options investments are generally more volatile, and may require more monitoring than investments in shares, there are a whole range of profitable option strategies in which you **cannot** lose more than your initial stake.

Once the basics have been learnt (and understood), you will find ways of using index options to turn movements in the markets into profits. The concept of an option is simple, but like all things, options and their related strategies can be made as complicated as you want. There are a whole range of options and strategies which you have probably never heard of, will never hear of and (quite frankly, as a private option investor), need not concern you.

Like all things, if you keep your feet firmly on the ground, apply common sense, and keep it simple, you may have more success than the 'professionals' who spend so much of their time making things perhaps more complicated than they should be. Incidentally, this is sometimes known in the profession as 'paralysis by analysis'.

Let's now take a closer look at options. There are basically (in the very broadest terms) two types of options:

- Call options.

- Put options.

Call options

We shall first deal with call options since they are easier to understand by beginners.

The formal definition of a call option is: **a financial asset whose value is derived from another financial instrument and which gives the owner the right (not the obligation) to *buy* the underlying financial instrument at a later time in the future for a price agreed today.** If this rather terse definition leaves you none the wiser, do not despair! The following analogy will help to further clarify the definition.

Suppose you wanted to buy a classic car whose price you believed was going to increase, and that you could 'secure' the item at an agreed sum (the current price) by paying a small, non-refundable deposit (£100 pounds) to a car dealer. Further assume that there was a time limit (six months) by which you had to decide whether you wanted to buy the item or not.

The agreement you have struck with the classic car dealer is an example of a call option.

Now to introduce some option terminology:

1. *The agreement you have with the seller of the car, in the world of options, is known as **a call option**, since it gives you (the holder of the option) the right to 'call' or buy the car at a later time.*

▲

2. *The small, non-refundable deposit you paid, in the world of options is given a fancy name: **the option premium.***

3. *The item (the car) you wanted to buy is known as **the underlying** – as this is the underlying asset you will receive if you decide to take on your right to buy the car.*

4. *The time limit you were given (six months), to decide whether you still wanted to buy the car or not, is known as the **life span** of the option. The exact date on which you lose your right to buy the car is known as the **expiry date.***

5. *Deciding to buy the car (within the life span of the option of course) is known as **exercising** the option. This is because you are exercising your right to buy the underlying (car).*

6. *The agreed price is known as the '**strike**' or '**strike price**'. It is also sometimes known as the **exercise price**. This is because it is the price at which you can exercise your right to buy the underlying item.*

The reason for the term 'call' is now becoming apparent: the owner of a call option can call away the underlying item (a classic car in this example) from the seller of the option contract.

One point to note is that the buying of an option contract conveys to the owner *merely a right* – not an obligation – to buy the underlying item. Therefore an option buyer can always 'walk away from the deal' (original option contract) if he/she decides against buying the underlying item (maybe there is new evidence that the price of the classic car was not going to increase after all – or the price may actually be falling). In this case, the option buyer will walk away and will lose his/her non-refundable deposit but will have no further obligations to the seller of the car. Although the full amount of the non-refundable deposit would have been lost (a 100% deficit), the absolute value of the loss will be small compared to actually buying the car ahead of an expected price increase, only to find that the price has fallen lower. However, if the price of the car were to increase by £2000, your original contract that you bought for £100 would be worth £2000. This illustration provides three important lessons about buying options:

- Options are high leverage instruments.

- You can never lose more than you invest when you BUY an option.

- Never invest more than you can afford to lose.

Put options

Much of what has been said for call options also holds true for put options. The only slight twist is that a put option is the reverse or mirror image of a call option, and so acts in the opposite direction. Don't worry if this statement is not too clear at this stage. An example similar to the one used above will illustrate the use of a put option more clearly.

However, before proceeding, let's quickly introduce the definition of a put: **a put option is a financial asset whose value is derived from another financial instrument and which gives the owner the right (not the obligation) to sell the underlying financial instrument at a later time in the future for a price agreed today.** As you can see from the definition, the only difference between a call and a put option is that a put option confers upon the owner of the put the right to **sell** the underlying item whereas the call option confers upon the owner of the call the right to **buy** the underlying item.

The following hypothetical scenario will help to clarify the definition of the put. Suppose you wanted to sell an item – a painting, say – whose price you believed was going to *decrease*, that you could find an antiques dealer somewhere who, for a small fee, will guarantee to buy the painting at an agreed price (the current price). Now let's say there was a time limit (six months) within which you had to decide whether you wanted to sell the painting or not. The agreement you have made with the antique dealer would be a perfect example of a put option. The terminology introduced in the call option section applies for put options as well (just substitute painting for classic car as the underlying).

The table below may help you to remember the differences between the two main option types:

Option Type:	Gives you the right to :
Call	BUY
Put	SELL

There is one last feature of options that is worth introducing at this stage. This concerns the *type* of exercise that the option has. For the sake of simplicity, we shall consider the two main exercise types (as far as private investors are concerned). They are namely:

American exercise

This type of exercise allows the owner of the option to exercise his/her option (ie. decide to buy or sell the underlying) on *any working day* during the life span of the option held.

European exercise

This type of exercise allows the owner of the option to exercise his/her option (ie. decide to buy or sell the underlying) on the *last working day* (ie. the expiry day) of the held option.

Using the earlier examples, if your call option was American style, then you could decide to buy the underlying (car) on any working day up to and including the expiry day. However, if it was European style, even if you decided to buy the underlying (classic car) earlier on, there wasn't anything you could do about it until the last (expiry) day.

Naturally, most people prefer the flexibility offered by American style options and they are therefore generally more expensive than European style options. For the remainder of the book, all references to options will refer to American exercise unless otherwise stated.

A **traded** option is an option that has the added benefit of being tradable. In other words, a holder of an option may decide to sell his/her option to another investor, thus conferring the right to buy or sell (depending on the type of option) to the new owner. It is this feature of traded options that allows them to be treated as an investment in their own right – that is, they can be bought and sold just like any other financial instrument (without having to exercise the right to trade in the underlying). In general, an option investor will sell his/her traded option to realise a profit or to cut a loss (just as with other traditional investments – shares, gilts etc.).

Normally, a call option's value will increase as the value (price) of the underlying rises and, similarly, decrease when the underlying's price falls. Therefore option investors normally buy calls when they believe the price of the underlying will increase. A put option, on the other hand, moves in the opposite direction to the underlying: an increase in the price of the underlying will cause the value of a put option to decrease and vice-versa.

Although it may seem strange at first, the definition of a put helps to explain this apparently 'peculiar' price behaviour.

Since a put option confers on the owner the right to sell the underlying at a certain price in the future, the put will be worth more as the price of the underlying falls further away from the put exercise price. The reason for this is that the put becomes worth more as the price of the underlying falls further away (this will be explained in greater detail in the section covering uses of options).

In addition to the put becoming more valuable, there is another factor that would help make the puts become more expensive. As a result of increased fear of a further fall in the price of the underlying, current holders of the underlying will want the put (for the right to sell their underlying at the higher price dictated by the put exercise price), and this increased demand manifests itself in the form of higher prices in the market. Option investors normally buy puts when they believe the price of the underlying will fall.

Options may be used to achieve several investment objectives including:

- Hedging (providing insurance against the fall in the value of a portfolio).

- Generation of further income by an owner of the underlying.

- Speculation.

Let's look at each of these in turn:

HEDGING: refers to the process of protecting one's holding. Hedgers are normally investors who have an investment in the underlying and therefore want to hedge their position against an adverse movement in the market (for the purposes of this book, we shall only consider long positions – see Glossary, page 163). For example, an investor may feel slightly bearish of

▲

the market after conducting analysis or research. Rather than completely liquidating his/her position and incurring high transaction costs (the initial analysis may also be wrong), it is far more prudent to insure the position by purchasing put options (as we shall see later).

INCOME GENERATION: There are several option strategies such as covered writes (which will be discussed later in this book) which allow an investor who owns the underlying (share for example) to achieve returns greater than that for the pure underlying holding alone.

SPECULATION: Speculators generally do not have an investment they want to protect or hedge – they merely use options as a medium to express an opinion on price movement and/or price direction. Options are high leverage assets and therefore huge profits can be realised (usually over a very short period) if the speculator's forecast is correct. However, the flip side of the coin is that the increased profit potential is associated with greater risks and speculators may also lose money (equally rapidly) if their forecasts are proved wrong by the market. If the option investor has not implemented a finite risk* strategy – that is when options suddenly bare their teeth at the unwary investor. Such an ill-prepared option investor may quickly find himself/herself with a loss several times greater than his/her initial 'stake'. This is how the second options myth (see page 18) is propagated – and why it is always recommended that option investors limit their option strategies to finite risk strategies until they are absolutely sure they know what they are doing.

* See Glossary on page 163

Some examples

Let's look at a few scenarios that will illustrate hedging and speculation using our previous classic car example:

Suppose that after you have done some preliminary research, you formed the view that a particular make of classic car which you owned was due to depreciate rapidly over the next few months. The rational thing for you to do would be to sell the car – fast! But what if your initial research was flawed, or in some way biased? Perhaps the 'research' was based on a snippet of a conversation overhead in your local pub. You would have sold a car which you probably did not want to sell, and could also run the risk of watching the value of your classic car actually appreciate! The sensible thing to do in this case would be to hedge your asset or long position (investment) in the classic car by buying put options on it.

The table on page 27 illustrates how you can be better off by hedging your position by buying a put option.

Case 1 – The classic car's price depreciates as forecast.

	Initial Cost	Resale Value	Profit (Loss)
Owner of car only			
Car component :	£10,000	£7,500	(£2,500)
Total Final Value = £7,500			
Owner of car + put option			
Car component :	£10,000	£7,500	(£2,500)
Put option component :	£200	£2,500	£2,300
Total Final Value = £9,800			

As you can see from the table above, the use of the put option has reduced the total loss on the car by 92%.

Let's take a closer look at what is actually happening. The assumptions made in the above table are that the put option cost £200 and gave you the right to sell your classic car at the strike price of £10,000. When the classic car's price fell from £10,000 to £7,500 – a loss of £2,500 – the put option became intrinsically worth £2,500. Why? It allows you to sell the underlying to the seller of the option (the car dealer in this case) at £10,000 (the strike price) whilst the underlying itself is readily available at £7,500 elsewhere. In practice, added demand will be generated by other owners of the underlying (classic car) who did not foresee the price fall, and who will now be clamouring for your put option (as a hedge – in case the price of the classic car dropped even further), sending the price even higher. So the phenomenal profit made on the put option offsets a large portion of the loss incurred by the fall in the price of the underlying (classic car in this case).

You may have noticed the similarity between the price paid for a put option (option premium) and 'ordinary' insurance premium as paid for home and contents, car theft etc. In fact, 'hedging' is just a fancy name for plain old insurance. Once again, we see how concepts and option terminology have a habit of cropping up in everyday life. There is nothing new under the sun — read on and find out more!

Now let's look at the alternative scenario:

Case 2 – The classic car's price does not depreciate as forecast.

	Initial Cost	Resale Value	Profit (Loss)
Owner of car only			
Car component :	£10,000	£10,000	£0.00

Total Final Value = £10,000

Owner of car + put option			
Car component :	£10,000	£10,000	£0.00
Put option component :	£200	£0.00	(£200)

Total Final Value = £9,800

The assumptions made in the above table are the same as those made in Case 1. As you can see from the table above, the use of the put option has resulted in a small loss (in percentage terms) on the holding. It is important to point out, however, that the amount lost on this occasion is in fact no more than the amount paid out as 'insurance premium' by buying the put option. Failure to hedge a position because of a fear of this small loss makes about as much sense as failing to insure your house against theft or fire because you have to pay an insurance premium.

▲

When the classic car's price failed to fall as predicted, at expiry of the put option (ie. on the last day you could exercise your right to sell the underlying), the put option will be worthless. Why? No one would want to pay you anything for a contract that is about to expire, certainly not for one that would give them the right to buy the underlying (car in this case) at £10,000 (the exercise price) when the underlying is freely available in the market at the **same** price of £10,000 (the exercise price of the put option).

Now let's take a look at speculation using options. We'll continue using our example of the classic car to gain a firm understanding of the uses of options, before moving on to real-life index option examples.

Suppose, after doing some research, you thought that a particular classic car's value was to drop substantially over the next few months. Let's further assume that you do not even own the classic car in question. You can, however, still benefit from a downward movement in the price of the underlying (car) by purchasing only put options. The table below illustrates this. The table is based on the same assumptions as made before, ie. the put option premium is £200 and the strike or exercise price is £10,000.

Case 3 – price of car falls as predicted.

	Purchase Cost	Sale Cost	Profit	% Gain
Put option :	£200	£2,500*	£2,300	1150%
Total			**£2,300**	**1150%**

** Assuming the price of the underlying (classic car) falls to £7,500.*

In this case you would have made an astonishing 1150% profit over the space of a couple of months. Since an option's maximum life span is 9 months, your annualised profit will be even more profitable.

Case 4 – price of car does not fall as predicted.

	Purchase Cost	Sale Cost	Profit (Loss)	% Gain (% Loss)
Put option:	£200	£0.00 *	(£200)	100%
Total			**(£200)**	**(100%)**

** At expiry, assuming the price of the underlying (classic car) remains unchanged, or moves above £10,000 (the exercise price).*

Now to consider the alternative scenario:

Once again, the maximum loss is limited to the amount you paid in the first instance, the option premium.

Before we look at hedging and speculation using index options, it is important to note the following slight (albeit important) difference between hedging and speculation. You hedge when you own the underlying but you can speculate regardless of whether you own the underlying or not. In the later part of this book, we shall be looking at several strategies that offer speculators opportunities to make money when the market is going up, down or is remaining relatively unchanged.

One point worth noting before the 'real life' case is discussed is that, in practice, options are bought and sold in units known as contracts, where one contract normally gives you the right to buy (or sell, depending on the kind of option) 1,000 of the underlying. Therefore, to be a more realistic example, our classic car option contracts described earlier would give us the right to buy not one classic car, but 1,000. This is an important point to note since it means that, in practice, you will have to multiply the option premium by 1,000 to find out what the initial cost per contract is.

We shall now look at hedging and speculation using index options.

HEDGING: Consider an investor who has a portfolio worth £20,000 in the market. We can say that the investor is *long of the market*, or has a *long position* in the market. This is all market jargon which basically means that the investor has got money invested in the market. Suppose this investor forms the opinion that the market is currently over-bought or over-valued and is likely to drop over the next three months (the investor in this case is said to have a bearish view of the market). The portfolio can be hedged against a fall in the market by the purchase of FTSE-100 index put options. Assume that the market is at a level of 3750 when the investor starts to feel bearish. He/she may buy one 3750 FT-SE 100 index put option contract at a premium of 50 **index points*** each (say). If the market falls to 3500 (a drop of around 6.7%), then the 'unhedged' portfolio can be expected to drop by a similar amount, ie. 6.7% or £1,333. The value of the put option would have increased quite considerably as a result of the relatively sharp drop in the level of the index. Let's assume the premium on the 3750 FT-SE 100 index puts are now quoted at 200 **index points**.

The initial cost of the purchased puts can be calculated as:
$$£(50 \times 10) = £500$$

The resale value of the put options (with the index at 3750) is:
$$£(200 \times 10) = £2,000$$

The table on page 32 illustrates the benefits of using a put option if the market falls as predicted.

**Note that index option premiums are quoted in index points (not pennies as in equity options) and also remember that each index point is worth £10.*

	Initial Value	Final Value	Profit (Loss)
'Unhedged' Position			
Portfolio:	£20,000	£18,667	(£1,333)
Final Total Value = £18,667			
Hedged Position			
Portfolio :	£20,000	£18,667	(£1,333)
Put option component :	£500	£2,000	£1,500
Final Total Value = £20,167			

Note that in this particular example, the 20-fold increase in the value of the put option has not only offset the loss on the portfolio, but has actually allowed the investor to realise a small profit – even though the overall market fell!

SPECULATING: Consider an investor who believes that the market is due to rise (the investor in this case is said to have a bullish view of the market) and thinks this will happen over the next six months. Assume that the market is at a level of 3750 in March when our investor starts to feel bullish. He/she then can take advantage of any rally in the market by purchasing FT-SE 100 index call options. Let's say the September (six months away) 3750 FT-SE 100 index call options are available for 35 **index points** each. Let's assume that sometime during the life of the option (August for example), the level of the index is 3800 and that the 3750 call options are now quoted at 60 **index points**. If the investor had previously bought two September 3750 FT-SE 100 index call options, then the profit that would have arisen from the speculative position taken can be analysed as follows:

Purchase price = £(2x35x10) = £700

Resale price = £(2x60x10) = £1,200

Purchase Price	Resale Price	% Gain
£700	£1,200	71.4

The table below illustrates the position if the market falls instead of rises. In the worst-case scenario described in the table below, the purchased calls will become worthless.

Purchase Price	Resale Price	% Gain
£700	£0.00	-100

In this case the whole of the initial or purchase price is lost, leaving the investor with a 100% loss. However, this is the maximum amount that the investor can lose. A well informed option investor, mindful of the risks and rewards available to him/her, only speculates with a proportion of his/her entire portfolio, and in undertaking a finite risk strategy such as this, is fully aware from the outset of the maximum possible loss.

Options and shares compared

Options differ from shares in many ways, the most obvious difference being that of gearing and flexibility. As mentioned several times before, with shares, investors only make money when the share price moves upward – and an investor in shares (in the absence of hedging) inevitably loses money when the price of the shares he has bought falls.

An option investor, however, can make money under the following scenarios (utilising the appropriate strategies):

1. *If the price of the underlying increases.*

2. *If the price of the underlying decreases.*

3. *If the price of the underlying does not move by any significant amount within a given time period.*

4. *If the price of the underlying stays within a predetermined price range within a given time period.*

5. *If certain anomalies exist in the options market (arbitrage opportunities).*

As you can see from the above, for every conceivable movement of the underlying, an option investor can make a profit by utilising an appropriate option strategy.

Another distinct difference between shares and options is the aspect of gearing. Options are high geared, high leverage financial instruments. The following example should illustrate this point further.

Suppose that in February, we have two investors (one an investor in company shares and another an option investor) who are both bullish on the shares of a particular company (ie. they believe the share price will increase). Further assume that the share is selling at 200p when they both decide to invest in the share. The share investor buys the underlying shares for 200p and the option investor buys an August 180 call option on the shares for 22p (remember that the call option effectively gives the option investor the right to buy the underlying share for 180p at any time up till expiry in August). If the shares then rise up to 260p in July (for example), the share investor would have a made a profit of 30%. The option investor, however, would have made a profit of 363.6%.

The table below illustrates how these figures are obtained:

	Initial Cost	Resale Cost	Profit	Percentage Gain
Investor in company shares	200p	260p	60p	30%
Option Investor	22p	(260p-180p) = 80p	(80p-22p) =58p	263.6%

With gearing, you can make enormous profits in a short time, using a very small initial stake. The flip side of the coin is that when things go wrong, you could lose your initial stake remarkably quickly. If you do not implement a finite risk strategy, you could end up losing more than your initial stake when the market proves you wrong. This is why option investors are always advised to implement finite risk strategies (see chapter six on option strategies), so that in the worst case possible, you only lose what you put down initially. You can 'walk away from the table', and live to fight another battle! Investing in the option instead of the underlying also had another advantage which may not be so obvious; the money that was 'saved' by not investing in the market (200p − 22p) = 178p could be earning interest in a high interest account.

The table on page 36 summarises the actions to be taken regarding your view of the underlying market. That is, if you believe the underlying is due to increase, then you would generally buy calls; similarly, if you expect the index to fall, then generally you would buy puts.

Option to buy	Underlying ↑	Underlying ↓
Call	✓	✗
Put	✗	✓

In later chapters we shall be looking at how we can combine these options to create other option positions and provide enough flexibility to cater for almost all investment objectives and market movements.

Here are a few more option terms. It is important that you understand what these terms mean since this knowledge will help you to understand some of the strategies described later on in the book, and will also help you to understand how to choose between various options.

1. *A call option whose exercise price is higher than the price of the underlying or a put option whose exercise price is lower than the price of the underlying is known as* **OUT-THE-MONEY.**

2. *An option whose exercise price is equal to the price of the underlying is said to be* **AT-THE-MONEY.**

3. *A call option whose exercise price is lower than the price of the underlying or a put option whose exercise price is higher than the price of the underlying is known as* **IN-THE-MONEY.**

If an option's exercise price is very far away from the price of the underlying, it is said to be *deeply* IN-THE-MONEY or *deeply* OUT-THE-MONEY as appropriate.

The table below might help to illustrate this important further subdivision of options. As we shall see later on in the book IN-THE-MONEY, AT-THE-MONEY and OUT-THE-MONEY have different characteristics or risk profiles which make them more suitable (or not as the case may be) for particular kinds of index option strategies and investor risk profiles.

	Exercise Underlying	Exercise = Underlying	Exercise > Underlying
Call Option	IN-THE-MONEY	AT-THE-MONEY	OUT-THE-MONEY
Put Option	OUT-THE-MONEY	AT-THE-MONEY	IN-THE-MONEY

An option's premium (market price) can be thought of as being made up of two components:

- Time premium.

- Intrinsic value.

An option will always have time value (you will always pay something, however small, for the right to exercise an option at some time in the future), though sometimes the intrinsic value of an option may be zero. In such cases, the option premium consists of time value only. Generally, the further dated (ie. the longer the life span of an option), the more expensive it will be. The intrinsic value of an option is the difference between the exercise price and the price of the underlying. Obtaining a negative value for a call option means that the call option has no intrinsic value. Similarly, because of the 'reverse' nature of a put option, obtaining a positive value indicates that the put option has no intrinsic value. The following table and the simple examples of both an equity and index option will illustrate this point.

	Time Value?	Intrinsic Value?
In-the-money option	✓	✓
At-the-money option	✓	✗
Out-the-money option	✓	✗

Suppose the current level of the FT-SE 100 is 3770, then the table below gives a few examples of the type of options in each category, as defined above.

Options can be further divided into classes. An option class refers to all options of the same type (ie. call or put) and based on the same underlying. Options belonging to the same option class and with the same exercise price and expiry date are known as an option series. Option series are necessary to avoid ambiguity when trading options. An example of an option series would be a March 3550 FT-SE 100 index call option. This particular option series refers to the call option available on the FT-SE 100 index, with a strike price of 3550 and which will expire in March. Index options always expire at 10:30 AM on

Option Series	IN-THE-MONEY	AT-THE-MONEY	OUT-THE-MONEY
3750 FT-SE 100 index call option	✓	✗	✗
4000 FT-SE 100 index put option	✓	✗	✗
3000 FT-SE 100 index put option	✗	✗	✓
2750 FT-SE 100 index call option	✓	✗	✗
4000 FT-SE 100 index call option	✗	✗	✓
3750 FT-SE 100 index put option	✗	✗	✓
3770 FT-SE 100 index put option	✗	✓	✗
3770 FT-SE 100 index call option	✗	✓	✗
3775 FT-SE 100 index call option	✗	✗	✓

the third Friday of the expiry month. An exchange calendar giving the exact expiry dates of all options is available from LIFFE (the London International Financial Futures and Options Exchange). This diagram will help further illustrate the various categories of options.

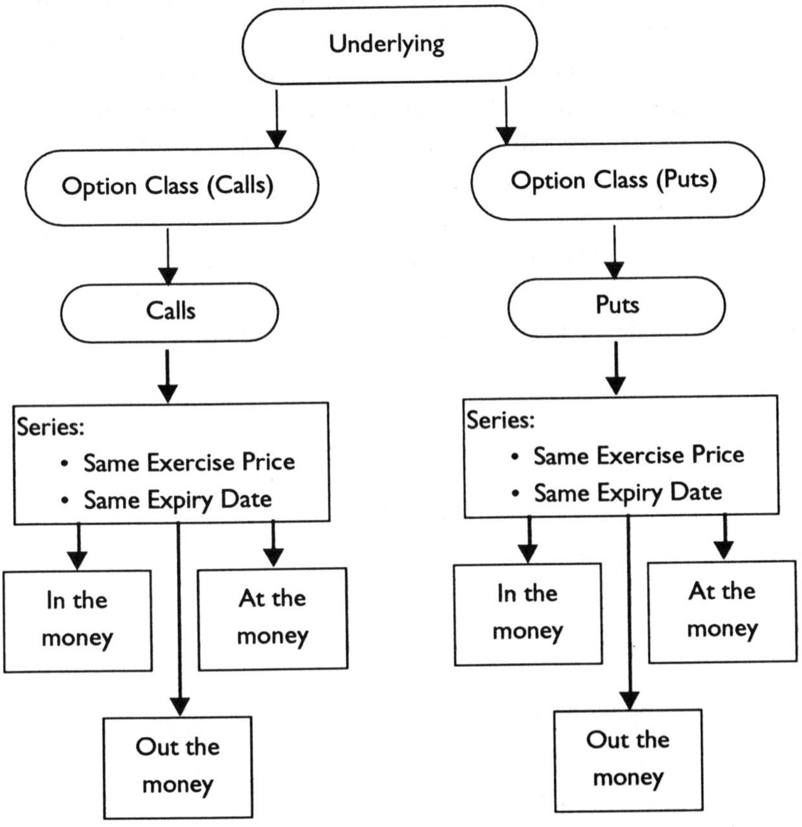

In practice, the underlying of the option will be a financial instrument and therefore may be an equity (a share), an index, a bond, a currency, a commodity (eg. sugar or gold), a future etc. This book will focus exclusively on index options. An index option (as the name may suggest) is an option that is based on an index: that is, an option that has an index as its underlying.

In the UK, the main index is the FT-SE 100 index. However, the concepts, ideas and strategies introduced and developed in this book are transferable and can be applied to a whole variety of other options.

You'll be glad to know that the option terminology introduced in this chapter constitutes a large proportion of what you need to know to understand options. Therefore, with our new arsenal of option terminology introduced in this section, we can set about investigating the option investment process more closely to see how a profit can arise in a traded index option investment. Since we shall be concentrating on the FT-SE 100 index (and the options based on it), it is important to introduce the FT-SE 100 and to look at how its level is calculated and what factors affect its value.

* * *

Chapter 2
THE FT-SE 100 INDEX

An index, in a very simplistic sense, is just a number. A share index is a number that is calculated in order to measure the value of a portfolio or 'basket' of shares. The FT-SE 100 is the UK's leading share index and is normally considered by investors as a proxy for the UK equity market. One may sometimes hear statements such as "The London market was up 20 points on the day" where it is the FT-SE 100 index that is being referred to as 'the market'. Also, when an investor or market professional asks, "How is the market doing?", he/she is usually referring to the FT-SE 100. So what is the FT-SE 100 index and why is it so important? The FT-SE 100 index (sometimes known as the 'Footsie') is an index of the largest one hundred companies (in terms of market capitalisation) in the UK. These companies (FT-SE 100 constituents) also have to qualify for inclusion in the index under special rules. The index was launched in 1984 and options based on the index were also first introduced in the same year.

In very simple terms, the FT-SE 100 index is an average of the prices of the shares of these 100 companies. The general idea behind bothering to keep track of the value of the shares of the largest 100 companies is that, on the whole, when these large companies do well (ie. when their share price increases), most of the smaller companies in the market generally tend to do well, and when the biggest companies don't do too well (ie. when their share price decreases), the smaller companies follow suit. Therefore, by keeping track of the value of the shares of the largest companies, investors get an idea of how the overall market is doing.

In many ways, it is less difficult to determine the likely behaviour of the overall market than it is to determine the behaviour of a particular company in the market. Companies are much more susceptible to all sorts of unpredictable shocks such as a company director resigning, profits warnings, take-over situations, or they may be classified in a particular sector that may suddenly declare a 'price war' rendering the whole sector 'unfashionable'. Although the FT-SE 100 is an average of several large companies, it would take several such irregularities or shocks to significantly move the level of the FT-SE 100 index. Consequently, the FT-SE 100 index is often much less volatile than the shares of its constituent companies. This is not to say that the FT-SE 100 is completely impervious to external factors. In fact there are several well known explanatory co-variables (factors such as movements in the Dow Jones Industrial Average, movements of the FT-SE 100 future and macro- and micro-economic perceptions and expectations to name but a few) that may have a direct impact on the behaviour of the FT-SE 100 index. A detailed discussion of how each of these factors influence the level of the FT-SE 100 index is outside the scope of this book.

The following is a list of some of the benefits or advantages of index options:

- There are many investors who are generally more successful at predicting the direction of the market as a whole than picking individual company outperformers (ie. they tend to pick companies that under-perform the market). Index options provide such investors with a tool for speculating on the direction of the overall market.

- As a result of their inherent high gearing, index options also offer a low cost way to buy into the market when cash is anticipated but not readily available.

- As a result of lower volatility of the underlying index, index options are often relatively cheaper than equity options.

- Additionally (as we shall see later), index options allow investors to hedge their portfolios against a possible fall in the value of their holdings.

The FT-SE 100 is calculated on a minute-by-minute basis by the London Stock Exchange. Its closing level (for the previous day) is readily available in the daily financial press. A slightly more up-to-date level of the index may be obtained on TELETEXT and real-time feeds for the index level are available from many data vendors.

Since index options are based on the FT-SE 100, to be able successfully to trade FT-SE 100 index options, it will be prudent to spend a little time investigating how the FT-SE 100 index is calculated.

There are three factors that should be most important to index option investors:

1. *How the index is calculated.*

2. *How dividends affect the level of the index.*

3. *The index constituents - (ie. which companies shares are used in constructing the index.)*

Let's first discover how the FT-SE 100 index is calculated. The FT-SE 100 index is an example of a weighted index. The NYSE composite, NASDAQ composite and S&P 500, which are all indices of American companies, are further examples of weighted indices. The method of calculation of the level of each of these indices is the same; it is only the constituent shares that are different.

Weighted indices

But what is a weighted index? A weighted index is just a fancy name given to the method of calculating an average (index). It is called weighted because each of the constituent shares is given a weighting, or significance, as a result of its market capitalisation. So, in effect, when the 'big boys' (the large capitalisation shares) move, the effect on the index is more dramatic than when a smaller capitalisation share moves. Once again, you may realise the importance of at least having an idea of some of the constituents of the FT-SE 100 (it really is not difficult to remember the constituent shares – most investors are already familiar with the companies as a large majority are household names), it takes only a couple of the large capitalisation companies to move in unison and several points can be added or knocked off the level of the index.

Now, let's look at how a weighted index is calculated. To calculate the level of such an index, you first find the market capitalisation of each of the constituent shares on a starting day (day 1). The market capitalisation M of a company is found by simply multiplying the current share price S by the number N of shares in issue.

Expressing this mathematically results in this not too fearsome expression:

$$M = S \times N$$

Now, you simply add together the market capitalisation of all the constituent shares in the index to find the total market capitalisation TotMkt. Once the total market capitalisation of the index on day 1 has been calculated, simply divide this value (TotMkt) by any number you want. This number is known as the divisor and is normally chosen to give the index a nice round number (usually 100 or 1,000) on its first day of creation. There – you have your own weighted index. The level of the index on subsequent days is calculated by finding the new market capitalisation and dividing by the same divisor.

Generally, once you have decided on a number for a divisor, you must not change the number again. However, adjustments are made to the divisor when companies are removed from the index due to merger and acquisition activity for example, or when a constituent company makes changes to its capitalisation by issuing more shares or by undertaking a share buy-back.

Let's now look at a numerical example that shows the construction of a hypothetical weighted index. Consider the following five hypothetical companies and their respective data. We shall construct an index based on these five companies and calculate the index on an additional two days.

Company	Number of shares in Issue	Price of share on Day 1 (p)	Price of share on Day 2 (p)	Price of share on Day 3 (p)
Doodah Group	1,000,000	130	128	132
Thingy Corporation	1,000,000	162	160	158
Watsit Plc	500,000	244	244	248
Widget & Co. Plc	2,500,000	336	345	350
Something Plc	750,000	108	90	96
Level of Weighted Index		1000.0	1003.7	1019.4

On day 1, the total market capitalisation of the index (ie. the sum of the market capitalisation of the constituent five companies) is

$$
\begin{aligned}
\text{TotMkt} \quad = \quad &(1{,}000{,}000 \times 130) + (1{,}000{,}000 \times 162) + \\
&(500{,}000 \times 244) + (2{,}500{,}000 \times 336) + \\
&(750{,}000 \times 108) \\
\\
= \quad &1{,}335{,}000{,}000
\end{aligned}
$$

A possible divisor to use would be 1,335,000 to give us a nice starting value of 1,000 for the index on day 1. To calculate the level of the index on day 2, we first find the total market capitalisation of the index (on day 2):

$$
\begin{aligned}
\text{TotMkt} \quad = \quad &(1{,}000{,}000 \times 128) + (1{,}000{,}000 \times 160) + \\
&(500{,}000 \times 244) + (2{,}500{,}000 \times 340) + \\
&(750{,}000 \times 90) \\
\\
= \quad &1{,}340{,}000{,}000
\end{aligned}
$$

The level of the index on day 2 is then calculated as

$$
\begin{aligned}
= \quad &(1{,}340{,}000{,}000) / (1{,}335{,}000) \\
\\
= \quad &1003.74
\end{aligned}
$$

Note that the level of the index has increased even though only one share price in the index has increased, the other shares either remained unchanged or even decreased! This is because Widget & Co. Plc is the largest in terms of market capitalisation and therefore changes in its share price will influence the level of the index more. Examples of FT-SE 100 index constituent companies with large market capitalisations are Glaxo-Wellcome, NatWest Bank and Shell. A percentage change in the share price of any one of these companies would have about the same effect on the level of the FT-SE 100 index as a 10% change in one of the smaller FT-SE 100 constituents.

The calculation of the level of the index for day 3 is as for day 2.

The effect of dividends

As you may already be aware, the price of shares decreases after they go ex-dividend, so if a number of large capitalisation constituents of the FT-SE 100 index go ex-dividend at around the same time, several points can be knocked off the value of the index. It may therefore be useful to know the ex-dividend days of some of the larger constituents (and possibly a figure of the dividends payable) so that you can calculate the likely level of the index (in the absence of external factors) when the shares have gone ex-dividend and see if there are any profitable strategies available. One such simple strategy could be to buy FT-SE 100 index put options before the expected drop in the level of the index (due to the constituent companies going ex-dividend). The level of option premiums available at the time (ie. whether options are 'cheap' or 'expensive') combined with your risk profile will determine which strategy (if any) will appeal to you. This is one example of how knowledge of how the index is calculated may be useful to an index option trader.

It is important to know (roughly at least), the companies used in the construction of the index and which sector classifications the various companies fall under. This information is particularly relevant if you intend to hedge your portfolio. The reason for this is that if the constituents of your portfolio are significantly different from the constituents of the FT-SE 100 index, your portfolio may not follow or 'track' the index closely enough and consequently, attempting to hedge the portfolio by using FT-SE 100 index options may not yield the expected results. Let me try to explain this further.

The table below gives the constituents of the FT-SE 100 and their weightings (explained later on in this chapter) as at 18 December 1995. The weighting of a company is very important. In an index it is a measure of the company's market capitalisation in comparison with the other constituent companies and therefore indicates its influence on the index – the larger the weighting, the larger the influence on the level of the index. The list is sorted by weighting in descending order.

Company Name	Sector	Weighting
Glaxo Wellcome PLC	Pharmaceuticals	5.15
British Petroleum PLC	Oil, Integrated	4.86
Shell Transport & Trading Co. PLC	Oil, Integrated	4.57
HSBC Hldgs (combined)	Banks, Retail	4.23
British Telecom PLC	Telecommunications	3.54
SmithKline Beecham (combined)	Pharmaceuticals	3.04
B.A.T. Industries PLC	Tobacco	2.78
Barclays PLC	Banks, Retail	2.04
Marks & Spencer PLC	Retailers, General	2.02
BTR PLC	Diversified Industrials	1.97
ZENECA Group PLC	Pharmaceuticals	1.94
NatWest Bank PLC	Banks, Retail	1.89
Lloyds Bank PLC	Banks, Retail	1.85
Unilever PLC	Food Producers	1.76
RTZ Corporation PLC	Extractive Industries	1.65
British Gas PLC	Gas Distribution	1.64
Reuters Holdings PLC	Media	1.63
Cable & Wireless PLC	Telecommunications	1.61
Hanson PLC	Diversified Industrials	1.59
Grand Metropolitan PLC	Alchoholic Beverages	1.55

Company Name	Sector	Weighting
Guinness PLC	Alcoholic Beverages	1.52
General Electric Co. PLC	Electronic & Electrical Eqpt	1.45
Abbey National PLC	Banks, Retail	1.37
Prudential Corporation PLC	Life Assurance	1.34
British Sky Broadcasting Group PLC	Media	1.16
THORN EMI PLC	Media	1.11
Sainsbury (J) PLC	Retailers, Food	1.10
Great Universal Stores PLC	Retailers, General	1.10
Vodafone Group PLC	Telecommunications	1.07
Bass PLC	Breweries, Pubs & Restaurants	1.04
Tesco PLC	Retailers, Food	1.03
TSB Group PLC	Banks, Retail	1.01
Standard Chartered PLC	Banks, Retail	0.91
Boots Co. PLC	Retailers, General	0.90
Reed International PLC	Media	0.90
Cadbury Schweppes PLC	Food Producers	0.88
Allied Domecq PLC	Alcoholic Beverages	0.87
Imperial Chemicals Group	Chemicals	0.87
National Power PLC	Electricity	0.85
Royal Bank of Scotland PLC	Banks, Retail	0.80
BAA PLC	Transport	0.79
British Airways PLC	Transport	0.74
BOC Group PLC	Chemicals	0.71
Commercial Union PLC	Insurance	0.68
Scottish & Newcastle PLC	Breweries, Pubs & Restaurants	0.62
PowerGen PLC	Electricity	0.61
Granada Group PLC	Leisure & Hotels	0.60
Rank Organisation PLC	Leisure & Hotels	0.60
Bank of Scotland (Governor & Co. of)	Banks, Retail	0.59
Kingfisher PLC	Retailers, General	0.57
Argyll Group PLC	Retailers, Food	0.57

Company Name	Sector	Weighting
National Grid Group PLC	Electricity	0.56
Pearson PLC	Media	0.56
Scottish Power PLC	Electricity	0.56
Siebe PLC	Engineering	0.55
British Aerospace PLC	Engineering	0.55
Tomkins PLC	Diversified Industrials	0.54
Legal & General Group PLC	Life Assurance	0.54
Rentokil Group PLC	Support Services	0.54
Associated British Foods PLC	Food Producers	0.53
Whitbread PLC	Breweries, Pubs & Restaurants	0.52
General Accident PLC	Insurance	0.52
Forte PLC	Leisure & Hotels	0.51
North West Water Group PLC	Water	0.51
Sun Alliance Group PLC	Insurance	0.51
British Steel PLC	Engineering	0.51
ASDA Group PLC	Retailers, Food	0.50
Land Securities PLC	Property	0.50
Reckitt & Colman PLC	Household Goods	0.47
Peninsular & Oriental Steam Navigation Co.	Transport	0.46
GKN PLC	Engineering, Vehicles	0.44
Rolls-Royce PLC	Engineering	0.42
Royal Insurance Holdings PLC	Insurance	0.41
RMC Group PLC	Building Materials & Merchants	0.41
Southern Electric PLC	Electricity	0.41
Wolseley PLC	Building Materials & Merchants	0.41
Schroders (combined)	Banks, Merchant	0.41
Severn Trent PLC	Water	0.40
3i Group PLC	Investment Trusts	0.40
Blue Circle Industries PLC	Building Materials & Merchants	0.39
Guardian Royal Exchange PLC	Insurance	0.39

Company Name	Sector	Weighting
Thames Water PLC	Water	0.37
Pilkington PLC	Building Materials & Merchants	0.36
Smith Industries PLC	Engineering	0.34
Cookson Group PLC	Diversified Industrials	0.34
TI Group PLC	Engineering	0.33
Redland PLC	Building Materials & Merchants	0.32
Enterprise Oil PLC	Oil Exploration & Production	0.31
Burton Group PLC	Retailers, General	0.31
Argos PLC	Retailers, General	0.31
Burmah Castrol PLC	Oil, Integrated	0.30
Williams Holdings PLC	Diversified Industrials	0.30
Tate & Lyle PLC	Food Producers	0.29
REXAM PLC	Paper, Packaging & Printing	0.29
Ladbroke Group PLC	Leisure & Hotels	0.28
F & C Investment Trust PLC	Investment Trusts	0.28
LASMO PLC	Oil Exploration & Production	0.28
Courtaulds PLC	Chemicals	0.26
Total *		**100.00**

**Note: weightings may not add up to exactly 100.00 due to rounding errors.*

A list of the constituents of the FT-SE 100 index is available from the London Stock Exchange (Tel: 0171 588 2355).

For the best results when hedging your portfolio, you should include as many FT-SE 100 constituent companies as possible and in the sector proportion that reflects the structure of the FT-SE 100. Failing that, the next best strategy would be to try to replicate what I call the 'sector structure' of the FT-SE 100 by using companies in the same sector as the FT-SE 100 index constituents. The term 'sector structure' refers to the proportion of the various industrial sectors as represented by the FT-SE 100. To calculate the 'sector structure' it is important to use a list such as the one above and sort all the companies by sector, then find the total weightings for each of the sectors. This will give you an idea of how much influence the various sectors have on the level of the index.

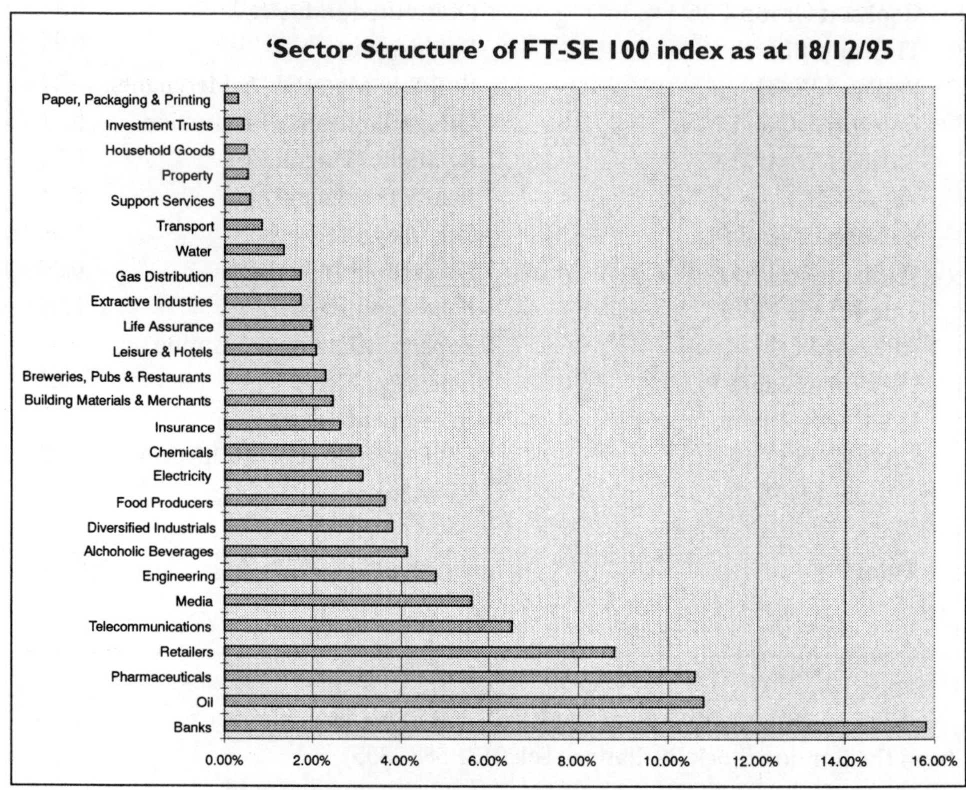

The chart shows the sector structure of the FT-SE 100 as at 18 December 1995. Remember that the FT-SE 100 list is not static and that companies are occasionally removed or added to the list over time (as a result of merger and take-over activity etc.). However, the overall total number of companies remains at 100. Changes in the list are not as rampant as you may think as since by definition of the rules, new entrants are historically healthy companies. A large majority of companies, once added to the list, strive to remain there (de-listing is the market equivalent of a public flogging). Consequently, several companies have remained on the FT-SE 100 index list ever since the index was introduced in 1984, and new entrants have mostly been added as vacancies have arisen as a result of mergers & acquisitions activity between the FT-SE 100 constituents. When a company is added to the FT-SE 100, the new company gains added prestige – if you like 'a market badge of success' – and its shares invariably rise as the large funds buy more to increase their portfolio weighting of the company, reflecting the role it now plays in the FT-SE 100 index. In other words, the large funds adjust their 'sector structure' so that their portfolios continue to 'track' the FT-SE 100 index as closely as possible.

The following example further illustrates the relevance of the 'sector structure' of an index. Assume there is a leading hypothetical market index comprising a 'sector structure' of 20% pharmaceuticals, 40% utilities, 10% retailers and 30% conglomerates. How would you ideally invest, in order to benefit from the hedging capabilities offered by put options on the hypothetical index? Ideally, what you should be aiming to do is to replicate the index in your portfolio, ie. the ideal portfolio should be a 'smaller version' of the index and should similarly be composed (in value terms) of 20% pharmaceuticals, 40% utilities, 10% retailers and 30% conglomerates if you would like to hedge your portfolio against a possible fall in the value of the index. The general idea is to create a portfolio that is as similar as possible to the index which represents the market in which the portfolio is invested. If you think about it, FT-SE 100 index put options are not going to offset many of your losses if the FT-SE 100 index dips by 10% and the value of your portfolio decreases by 50%. This can happen if your portfolio does not 'track' or 'follow' the FT-SE 100 index closely enough (in other words if you have selected the shares in your portfolio in an ad-hoc manner without paying attention to the 'sector structure' of the FT-SE 100 index). From the sector structure of the FT-SE 100 given above, it should be obvious that a portfolio that does not try to achieve a similar sector structure and has a large percentage (in value terms) of its holdings in the less significant sectors such as Investment Trusts or Household Goods is not likely to track the FT-SE 100 very closely. Several investors are not aware of the 'sector structure' of the index although, as you can see from the above discussions, it is paramount to successful hedging – and is worth the extra time spent in understanding it.

Construction of a 'hedgeable' portfolio

From what has been said above, your portfolio should 'track' the FT-SE 100 index as closely as possible if you want to hedge it using FT-SE 100 index put options. This begs the question "how does one go about constructing a portfolio that follows or 'tracks' the FT-SE 100 index as closely as possible?". Your starting point is to be aware of the sector structure of the FT-SE 100 index (I have included a chart on page 52 of the FT-SE 100 index as at 18 December 1995 for these purposes). From the chart, you can clearly see the sector structure of the FT-SE 100 index. So, ideally, you know that your portfolio should be split in the same proportion (in terms of value) across the sectors. Once you have identified the sectors (and their corresponding percentages), the next step would be to select companies within the sectors that have the highest **positive correlation** with the movements of that sector within the FTSE. What I mean is that you should make sure that if the Pharmaceuticals sector (for example) in the FT-SE 100 index increases by 5% then the

Pharmaceuticals sector in your portfolio would also increase by a corresponding 5% (and vice versa). The easiest way to do this is to select stocks that have the biggest weighting (ie. influence) within the Pharmaceuticals sector of the FT-SE 100 index. For example Glaxo Wellcome, Zeneca and ICI account for a very significant percentage of the movement of the Pharmaceuticals sector within the FT-SE 100 index, therefore by including these three companies in the Pharmaceuticals sector of your portfolio, your Pharmaceuticals sector is going to track the Pharmaceuticals sector of the FT-SE 100 very closely. By repeating this strategy across all the sectors, you will end up with a portfolio that is highly **positively correlated** with the FT-SE 100, which is exactly what you want if you want to hedge your portfolio using FT-SE 100 index options. The steps described above are summarised below:

- Be aware of the 'sector structure' of the index you want to hedge your portfolio against (eg. the FT-SE 100).

- Attempt to replicate the sector structure in your portfolio either by:

    a) Performing a correlation analysis on changes in the share price of a sector component company and changes in the value of the sector in the FT-SE 100 (this is particularly useful if you want to include **non FT-SE 100** companies in your portfolio);

OR by:

    b) Constructing the sectors of your portfolio by selecting the most dominant (influential or large weighted) FT-SE 100 companies falling in that sector classification.

The amount by which a portfolio 'tracks' an index is known as the beta. A portfolio that exactly mirrors the movements of the index is said to have a beta of 1.0. The further away the beta of your portfolio is from 1.0, the more you will have to resort to complicated methodologies to successfully hedge your portfolio against a fall in the index. A detailed discussion of hedging a portfolio which does not exactly mirror the movements of the FT-SE 100 is outside the scope of this book.

Index option *speculators*, however, do not have to be overly concerned about the individual constituents of the index though a general knowledge of the sector structure of the index may help in making better predictions of the movements in the index. For example, if a hypothetical index has a sector structure of 80% Retailers and 20% Breweries, there is some merit in thinking along the lines that the index is likely to increase shortly after Christmas as a result of increased shopping during the Christmas period (assuming that this is when most of the constituent companies announce their results).

Some index option trading terms

Now to introduce a few useful terms to the index option trader:

- Tick size.

- Delivery month.

- Settlement price.

- The daily settlement price.

- EDSP.

The **TICK SIZE** is the minimum amount by which the level of the index is allowed to change by the exchange. Even though the index is a calculated number and therefore can assume any value, it is always rounded up and quoted to one decimal place. For the purposes of index options, the recognised minimum movement of the index is one half of a full index point, ie. 0.5. Every half point of movement of the FT-SE 100 index is worth £5.00.

DELIVERY MONTH refers to the expiry month of the index option. Unlike equity (stock) options which have series available with three month intervals (eg. January, April, July, October), index options are always available for June and December plus such additional months that the nearest four calendar months are always available for trading. So if the current month is February (say), then there will be FT-SE 100 index options available for June and December, as well as for February, March, April and May. Index options expire at 10:30 on the third Friday of the expiry month. Normally, on the last (expiry) day, there is a flurry of activity in the options market as traders close open positions, roll positions forward or try to make arbitrage trades (this terminology will be discussed in the trading in index options section). This has the effect of large volumes of trade going through the market up until the last hour of expiry of an option series which has been dubbed the 'triple witching hour'.

The **DAILY SETTLEMENT PRICE** is simply the level of the FT-SE 100 index at 16:10pm. If an option which is not yet due for expiry (ie. a non-expiring series) is exercised by its holder, then the level of the index used in the cash settlement will be the daily settlement price, which is the level of the FT-SE 100 index at the end of the trading day (4:10pm GMT). The following numerical example illustrates further:

Suppose you purchase the June 3500 calls and then wish to

exercise them (before expiry), when the level of the index is 3550 (say) at the close of business. The amount you will receive can be calculated as follows:

$$(3550 - 3500) = 50 \text{ index points}$$

From the specifications given in the (American) FT-SE 100 index option (see table opposite), each index point is worth £10. Therefore the cash receivable will be £500 (per index option contract).

The **EXCHANGE DELIVERY SETTLEMENT PRICE** (EDSP) is slightly different in its method of calculation and is only used for options that are expiring ie. options being exercised on their last day. The EDSP is based on the average level of the FT-SE 100 index between 10:10am and 10:30am on the last trading day. It is simply an arithmetical average of all the values that the index attains during this time interval, with the three highest values and three lowest values excluded from the calculation. The logic behind trimming off the extreme values is to minimise the effect that any large one-off transactions (remember the triple witching hour) may have on the calculated EDSP.

The interval between exercise prices is determined by the time to maturity of a particular expiry month and is either 50 or 100 index points. Additional exercise prices will be introduced on the business day after the underlying index level has exceeded the second highest, or fallen below the second lowest, available exercise price. The FT-SE has been known to move by as much as 50 points in a day. If you have been on the 'right' side of a movement in the index a 50 point move would be translated to an increase in your investment of £(50x10) = £500. Later on in this book I'll show you a couple of profitable index option strategies that you may try out for yourself. Only finite risk strategies will be discussed, for the benefit of inexperienced option investors.

The table below gives the specification for the American style index option.

Unit of Trading	Valued at £10 per index point
Delivery Months	June and December plus such additional months that the nearest four calendar months are always available for trading.
Exercise/Settlement Day	Exercise by 16:31 on any business day, extended to 18:00 for expiring series on the last trading day. Settlement day is the first business day after the day of exercise/Last trading day.
Last Trading (Expiry) Day	10:30 on the third Friday of the expiry month.
Quotation	Index points
Minimum Price Movement (Tick size & value)	0.5 (£5.00)
Trading Hours	08:35 – 16:10

For completeness (and comparison), a table is included overleaf, detailing the specifications of European index options. European style index options are mostly used by fund managers for hedging their portfolios against a fall in the market. The delivery months in the table show that the series are available for every quarter, and are therefore very useful

▲

for 'window dressing' – hedging against the value of the portfolio falling below a certain level – just in time for quarterly reviews or reports etc.

The table below gives the specification for the European style index option.

Exercise/Settlement Day	Exercise by 18:00 for expiring series on the last trading day. Settlement day is the first business day after the last trading day. (This option can only be exercised on the last trading day.)
Last Trading Day	10:30 Third Friday of the expiry month.
Quotation	Index points.
Minimum Price Movement (Tick size & value)	0.5 (£5.00).
Trading Hours	08:35 – 16:10.
Unit of Trading	Valued at £10 per index point.
Delivery Months	March, June, September and December plus such additional months that the nearest three calendar months are always available for trading.

One major difference between index options and equity options is that FT-SE 100 index options are cash settled when exercised. Whereas equity options have an underlying share which can be delivered by the seller of the option (for all practical purposes), there is no such physical entity that can be delivered to an index call option holder who decides to exercise his index call option. The reason for this is that it is impractical to deliver all the underlying 100 shares of the index. So, settlement is done with cash only. What this means is that when a FT-SE 100 index option is exercised, the owner receives a cash amount equal to the difference between the strike price of the option and the daily settlement price or EDSP (as the case may be). For this reason, index options are also known as contracts for differences.

As a private investor, index options provide a way for you to minimise your downside risk (ie. index options minimise the maximum loss possible on your portfolio). The following hypothetical scenario will illustrate this point further.

Suppose you have a diversified portfolio worth £350,000 which mirrors exactly* the movement of the FT-SE 100. Further assume that the current level of the FT-SE 100 index is 3500. Since each index point is worth £10, your portfolio is worth (350,000/3500x10) ie. 10 times the index. Using put options, you can actually decide the maximum loss on your portfolio that you are willing to tolerate, and implement a hedge by buying FT-SE 100 index options.

Let's look at how such a hedge can be implemented. Suppose you do not want the value of your portfolio to fall below £343,000 (representing a fall of 2% or £7,000). Since your portfolio 'follows' the movements of the FT-SE 100 index exactly, a decrease of 2% in the value of your portfolio will be brought about by an equivalent 2% decrease in the level of the index, which will bring the level of the index down from 3500 to 3430. Since you do not want to lose any more money if the index falls below this level (ie. if the market falls further), then you should buy put options with an **exercise price** at this level (ie. 3430). Additionally, since your portfolio is worth 10 times the value of the index (remember, each index point is worth £10), you need to buy 10 index put options to fully cover the value of your holding. So to effect a hedge that will stop the value of your portfolio from becoming less than £343,000 you must buy 10 x 3430 FT-SE 100 index options. The combined value of your put option and share portfolio will then *never* drop below £343,000 (during the life of the purchased put option) regardless of how low the FT-SE 100 index falls. It really is as simple as that!

Where to find FT-SE 100 index option quotes

The simplest and cheapest way of following the price of a particular index option series (assuming you don't have a broker) would be to obtain them by reading the financial press. One such source is the *Financial Times*.

LIFFE traded index (and equity) options are listed in the companies and markets section of the *Financial Times* from Tuesday to Saturday and are also available on CEEFAX (BBC 2). If the particular series you happen to be following does not appear in the *Financial Times* (or other publication), it does not mean that they have disappeared! These publications do not list the very deep in-the-money and very deep out-the-money options (to prevent having to print several pages of option prices). The option prices quoted are those closest to the current level of the FT-SE 100 index. In these instances, the prices for those series will be available from the CEEFAX pages – or from a broker, who will have access to real-time option prices.

**Note: in practice, most portfolios do not exactly mirror movements of the FT-SE 100, for the reasons discussed earlier. If you intend to hedge your portfolio against a fall in the market, it helps if your portfolio at least has a resemblance to the FT-SE 100 index as this will mean it tracks the FT-SE 100 index more closely.*

How to read option prices from the financial pages

The table below shows how option prices are reported in the financial pages of most national newspapers:

FT-SE 100 INDEX OPTION (LIFFE) (*3736) £10 per full index point

	3650		3700		3750		3800		3850	
	C	P	C	P	C	P	C	P	C	P
Mar	102.5	11	62.5	21	30	39.5	11.5	72	2.5	118
Apr	116	34	84.5	52	56.5	74.5	34.5	102.5	20	128
May	139	51.5	108	70.5	80.5	92.5	56	119	38.5	151.5
Jun	158.5	67	126	84.5	99.5	107.5	75.5	133.5	56.5	164.5
Dec ⚹			216.5	145			167.5	194		

⚹ *Long dated expiry months,* * *Underlying index level*

The first row indicates the various strike or exercise prices (remember that this is not an exhaustive list of all the exercise prices available), and the first column indicates the various expiry months available. As you may have guessed, the tags C and P in the second row denote call and put respectively. The asterisk preceding the value 3736 indicates the level of the index at the time of construction of the table.

Suppose, then, that we wanted to know the value of a May 3800 put. We can look it up in the table above by looking up the May row, and the 3800 Call column which gives us the value of 119 index points. One contract of the May 3800 FT-SE 100 index put option will then cost £(119 x 10) = £1,190.

It is important to be aware that the prices published in the financial press are a day old and are merely mid prices (ie. between the bid and ask prices). In practice, a bid and ask spread exists (ie. the buy price or **ask** will be different from the sell or **bid** price). The mid prices quoted are for indicative purposes only and should not be relied on for trading. Prices quoted on CEEFAX, though slightly preferable to the ones obtained through daily publications, are not real-time (ie. not live) and prices are only updated a couple of times a day – this may not be suitable for the more serious option investor. Options can be quite volatile at times and prices that are a day old (or even several hours old) may not be an accurate indicator of present market prices. Several live (real-time) exchange data vendors operate in the UK and so the more serious option investor is able to have access to real-time option prices if he/she should so wish.

Where and how are FT-SE 100 index options traded?

FT-SE 100 index options and several other options are traded on the London International Financial Futures and Options Exchange (LIFFE), the main options exchange in the UK which was formed as a result of a merger between the London traded options market (LTOM) and the London International Financial Futures and Options Exchange.

FT-SE 100 index options are traded by open outcry which means that index options are bought and sold by individuals (known as pit traders) who communicate directly with each other (on a face-to-face basis) by means of various hand signals. You'll be glad to know that you neither have to learn the cryptic hand signals to communicate with other pit traders nor even go to the trading pits to trade options. The way to trade options is through a broker. There are several such brokerage firms listed in LIFFE publications who will be more than willing to take your buy and sell instructions and pass them on to a floor trader for execution in the LIFFE pits. A large number of these brokers either have a presence on the floor (ie. they have employees who work on the LIFFE trading floor), or use the floor brokers of another firm, so that your orders can be executed instantly or as soon as possible. A list of such brokers is available from LIFFE (0171 379 2486).

Open outcry trading in options contrasts with dealing in shares. Dealing in shares is screen-based, ie. there is no face-to-face contact between the traders, and trades are conducted via screen-based quotes. The FTSE-100 Index Options market is open for trading between 8:35am and 4:10pm on weekdays.

* * *

Chapter 3
EVALUATING OPTIONS

The precise evaluation of options can be a complicated science. It is not the purpose of this book to delve into the underlying theory and equations of option pricing. However, like all things being traded (ie. bought and sold), in order to make a profit or even break even, one must have an idea of a 'fair value' of the item being bought or sold, as this will help in determining if the item is overpriced or underpriced. So how does one go about discovering the 'fair price' of an option without getting bogged down with the accompanying rocket science mathematics?. One quick and dirty way of doing this is to treat the option premium as being composed of a time value component and an intrinsic value component as described earlier. By comparing several series, an investor may then decide on 'gut feelings' that a particular series 'appears cheap' because he/she would not be paying too much time premium for the particular series, or that another option appears 'expensive' because 'there is too much time value'. Such a method, though it has its merits (and is used by a number of option investors), also has significant drawbacks – the most obvious one being subjectivity. In other words, one investor's guts may tell him/her a particular series was 'cheap' whereas another investor would find the same series outrageously expensive.

One way to inject some objectivity into pricing options would be to take a slightly closer look at the option and some of its properties and try to quantify these properties without getting too technical. Let's first look at the factors that determine the value of an option.

The direction in which the underlying market moves will have a significant effect on the value of an index option, ie. the profitability or otherwise of an index option position. As we saw earlier on, an investor in the underlying will only be interested in the direction of the market. Option traders, however, have at least one other factor to consider – the *speed* at which the underlying moves in a particular direction. While the option trader is sensitive to directional movements of the underlying (eg. FT-SE 100 index), he/she must also give careful consideration to the speed at which the change in the index is likely to occur. The speed of movement of the underlying (FT-SE 100 index in our case) is known as **volatility** and is the most important determinant of an option's price, as it is a direct reflection of the riskiness of the option to the option writer. The more volatile an underlying is, the riskier it is for the option writer since the underlying could move swiftly in an unexpected direction causing the option writer unlimited losses. So, for taking on the greater risk involved with writing an option on a volatile underlying, the option writer will seek a higher premium. The greater the volatility of the underlying, the more expensive the option based on it. Volatility is such an important factor in determining the fair price of an option that the whole of the next chapter will be devoted to discussing it.

The following example will impress on you just how important volatility is to an option trader. Suppose a futures trader and an option trader (both being bullish of the market) decide to take long positions in the FT-SE 100 index (ie. to buy a FT-SE 100 index future and a FT-SE 100 index call option respectively). If the market moves to a higher level, the futures trader will make a profit whereas the profitability of the option trader is not so assured. The reason for this is volatility. Do not let this put you off. Volatility is both friend and foe to the option trader and must be understood well by the serious option investor – in order to let it work for him/her. If the underlying index fails to move fast enough to offset the natural decay of the option (remember that an option is a decaying asset with a finite life span), then the option investor may actually incur a loss – even though the underlying index moved in the direction the investor had anticipated. This is the main reason why inexperienced option traders generally lose money in their first few trades, as they are lured by the prospect of infinite rewards and limited risk offered by certain option strategies and do not undertake any option analysis, therefore exposing themselves to unnecessary risk. It is my intention in this book to show you how to evaluate options before making investment decisions.

To successfully evaluate an option, you must have a good working knowledge of the basic characteristics of options, ie. what factors determine the price of an option and how the price of an option varies in changing market conditions. This knowledge forms the building blocks to understanding various investment strategies and their relative advantages and/or disadvantages. Armed with this knowledge, you can then make more informed choices when selecting an option (or set of options) to achieve a particular investment objective. It is worth pointing out at this stage that there is no such thing as the best strategy as different investors have different investment objectives and risk profiles (degrees of aversion to risk).

The concept of 'fair value' – what determines an option's theoretical value

An option has a theoretical or 'fair' value. This theoretical value can be calculated using a variety of pricing models. There are several different mathematical pricing models used to determine the theoretical price of an option, the most popular being the Black-Scholes model. The Cox-Ross-Rubinstein Binomial is another pricing model (more accurate for American style options) but is much more difficult to compute. It is well worth noting that software packages such as the Option Evaluator™ (included with this book) make the analysis of options extremely easy and accessible to the private investor.

The fair value of an option can indicate whether it is overpriced or underpriced in the market – and by how much it is **theoretically** mis-priced. It is useful to point out at this stage that you must be aware of the limitations of mathematical models. Mathematical models are just that – ie. *models* – they cannot possibly tell you everything there is to know about the market. For instance, instead of going ahead and buying an option merely because it is theoretically underpriced and therefore looks 'cheap' – ask yourself why that option is so cheap (in fact the cheaper it looks, the more suspicious you should be – **assuming, of course, that you have fed the correct parameters into the model)** – it could be that the market knows something you don't know yet. The cheapness of an equity option could be reflecting common knowledge of an imminent resignation of the chairman of the company or that the company may be due to announce a profit warning or even reveal particularly bad results. Similarly, do not sell options (selling options is particularly dangerous to the novice private investor at the best of times) simply because the series is theoretically overpriced – it could well be that the 'market' knows that the company is about to be a take-over target. It is unrealistic to expect a mathematical model to alert you if an imminent bad result is responsible for the 'cheapness' of an option.

Having said that, mathematical pricing models are a potent weapon in an option investor's arsenal, providing invaluable assistance when selecting series so that, all things being equal, they can help tilt the odds in your favour and also help you select options and strategies that are compatible with your risk profile. Every option investor must have a means of evaluating an option before embarking on a trade. We shall devote the whole of Chapter 5 to discussing how to analyse options using a PC and how to use the option analysis software pack included with this book.

The price of an index option is determined by the following:

1. *The level of the index.*

2. *The exercise or strike price of the option.*

3. *The rate at which the level of the index changes (known as volatility).*

4. *The time to expiry of the option.*

Ideally, these determinants should be quantified – ie. be given numerical values and then fed into a pricing model which would then generate the theoretical or 'fair value' of the option. By comparing this 'fair value' to the market price, investors can then generally determine if the option is overpriced or underpriced – mindful of what has been said earlier, it is often profitable to sell overpriced options and buy underpriced options (novice option investors are **strongly advised against** naked writes). This kind of trading is a form of 'arbitrage'. With the advent of option pricing software, it is possible for option investors to instantaneously calculate the fair value of an option along with other option parameters (discussed later) without manual effort.

To understand the concept of 'fair value', we must first look at an important statistical concept which always crops up in option pricing – the **'expectation'** or, in this context, **'expected return'**. Let me try to explain this further. Suppose you agree to play a dice tossing game with me. The rules of the game (initially) are that I will pay you the sterling amount equal to the number that comes up every time you throw the dice. That is, you win £3 (say) when, after rolling the dice, the number 3 comes up. Similarly, you will win £1 or £6 if the numbers 1 or 6 come up when you roll the dice. On average, you can *expect* to receive £3.5 per roll of the dice (assuming that we don't get tired of this game and play it an infinite number of times). How did I arrive at the number 3.5? Well, since all the numbers on the dice (1-6) have an equal chance of coming up, If we add up the six possible outcomes 1+2+3+4+5+6 and divide by 6 (the number of faces on the dice), we get 3.5. This is the amount that, on average, that you should **expect** to obtain each time you rolled the dice (in the long run). This is known as the **expected return**. In this case this will also be the 'fair value' of the dice.

To make this analogy more interesting (and closer to real life), I'll change the rules slightly (in my favour of course!). I will now charge you for the privilege of rolling the dice. That is, you will pay me a fixed amount each time, *before* you roll the dice. Since you expect to receive £3.5 for the right to toss the dice, if I charge you less than £3.5 each time the dice is rolled, you should still expect to make a profit in the *long run*. If I charge you £3.5 for the right to throw the dice, you should expect to break even in the *long run*. However, if I decide to charge you more than £3.5 for the right to toss the dice, then in the *long run*, you should expect to incur a loss. It is important to

▲

realise the phrase 'long term' which has statistical meaning. You cannot expect to receive £3.5 when you roll the dice only once (in fact this is an impossibility since the number 3.5 does not appear on any of the six faces of the dice). This little trivial game explains the concept of fair value. One can almost think of fair value as a sort of average.

The concept of fair value is crucial to successful option investment. As we have discovered, by paying less than the fair value, it is possible to get the laws of probability stacked in your favour (ie. you can expect to make a profit in the long run). You may also have noticed the similarities between the following:

1. *The price paid for the right to 'toss the dice' and the option premium.*

2. *The expected return and the theoretical or fair 'value' of an option.*

In the second version of the game, where I decide to charge you money for the privilege of playing, I am, in effect, playing the role of a market maker (or the other side of an option trade). Unsurprisingly, in real life you are not likely to find any-one who will be willing to charge you less than the expected or fair value. In fact you are more likely to be charged more than the 'fair value' to participate in the game. The difference between the premium asked and the expected value represents the potential profit or 'edge' the other player has over you in this hypothetical scenario.

So what is an option investor to do? You will be glad to know that all is not doom and gloom and that there are ways in which an option investor may tilt the probabilities in his/her favour and we will be taking a closer look at these various ways in the next section.

The other factors affecting an index option's theoretical price are the level of the index, time to expiry and the volatility of the index. The time to expiry obviously has an effect on the option price. As one would expect, the longer the time to expiry, the more expensive the option would be as, in gambling parlance, it would mean you have a greater chance of striking it lucky as the laws of probability start to tilt in your favour if you play for a long time. The table below illustrates how an option's price is affected by the factors described above:

	Call Option	Put Option
Index Level Increases	Price tends to increase	Price tends to decrease
Index Level Decreases	Price tends to decrease	Price tends to increase
Lower Exercise Price	Tends to be more expensive	Tends to be cheaper
Higher Exercise Price	Tends to be cheaper	Tends to be more expensive
Increasing Volatility of Index	Price tends to increase	Price tends to increase
Decreasing Volatility of Index	Price tends to decrease	Price tends to decrease
Short Time to Expiry	Tends to be cheaper	Tends to be cheaper
Long Time to Expiry	Tends to be more expensive	Tends to be more expensive

Calculating the riskiness of an option

To be successful in option trading, you have to be able to select options by more than just 'gut feelings'. Professional traders use a couple of risk measures (known in the profession as 'greeks' – because of their names). Don't be put off by their fanciful terms, they are really quite simple to understand.

These risk measures enable an option investor to tilt the probability of a profit in his/her favour. There are five main risk measures of options which are important in varying degrees to the option investor. They are:

1. *Delta.*

2. *Gamma.*

3. *Vega.*

4. *Rho.*

5. *Theta.*

It is this aspect of options (option pricing and sensitivities) that normally strikes fear into the heart of most option investors without a mathematical background. This need not necessarily be so. There is no need for formal proofs or equations in this book. There is a plethora of books available on the mathematics of pricing options and readers with a mathematical background (prerequisites being calculus and numerical analysis) will have several books to choose from. In this chapter, we discuss each of these sensitivities in a clear user-friendly and jargon-free language accessible to private investors and also look at a few practical examples illustrating how you can make use of these risk measures in every-day trading without getting bogged down by technical details. The increasing availability of option pricing software makes the computation of these risk measures child's play. It is really the interpretation of the values (rather than the computation) that is important. The value of the greeks normally ranges from 0 to 1 but is sometimes expressed in percentage form, ie. from 0 to 100.

Now, let's look at each of the risk measures individually and see what they mean, and how they can be used by option investors. We shall start with the most widely known and easiest to understand – the delta.

DELTA*

This is a number which indicates by how much an option's value will change if the underlying index moves by one point. The delta of an option provides the option investor with a measure of the sensitivity of the option with respect to a point change in the underlying. For an index option, the delta would tell us by how much the price of the index option will increase (decrease) if the level of the FT-SE 100 index increases (decreases) by one index point. The delta of an option can also be thought of as an approximate measure of the probability of the option expiring in-the-money. An option with a delta of 0.75 can be thought of as having a 75% probability of expiring in-the-money (**not necessarily profitable**).

Deep in-the-money calls have a delta of plus one, deep out-the-money calls have a delta close to zero and an at-the-money call has a delta of approximately 0.5. What this means is that if you have a deep in-the-money call option, for every 1 point movement that the index makes, your option will make a corresponding move in the same direction of 1 point. If the FT-SE 100 index is at 3700 for example, then a 3500 FT-SE 100 index call is deep in-the-money. Suppose such a call sells for about 210p. If the index rises by 10 points to 3710, the 3700 call will similarly gain by 10 points, and will therefore be worth 220p.

Put options always have a negative delta value – this is because a put option moves in the opposite direction to that of the underlying share, ie. an increase in the price of the underlying will result in a decrease of the value of the option

---

*__*Note:__ investors with a knowledge of calculus may be interested to know that the delta is the first partial derivative of the price of an option with respect to the price of the underlying.*

and a decrease in the price of the underlying share will result in an increase in the value of the option. Once again, deeply in-the-money put options have a delta of minus one, close to zero for an out-the-money put and approximately minus 0.5 for an at-the-money put. These numbers are important to an option investor because they indicate how much of an increase or decrease in the option price can be expected for short-term moves by the underlying stock and can therefore help in selecting an option. For example, a call with a delta of 0.75 can be expected to change in the same direction as the underlying by 75% for every one point move in the underlying. Put option values will always move in the opposite direction to the underlying.

Investors may wrongly conclude that in-the-money options are always the best choice, given a number of option series to select from. Even though this tends to be the case most of the time (ie. in-the-money options are a safer bet), this is not always the case and an investor must employ other selection criteria to be able to ascertain the option most likely to appreciate within the period of investment. Other factors must therefore be taken into account before selecting the option strategy that best suits an investor's objectives and risk profile. Generally speaking, though, it is relatively safer to invest in in-the-money options even though the return on investment will be much smaller than that of a successful out-the-money option purchase.

It is important to note that the delta of an option (or combined option position) is not constant and is dependent on the price of the option itself and its time to expiry among other factors. One of the more important features of the delta is the way it changes over the life of an option. The delta tends to decay more rapidly towards the end of an option's life. It is very important for option investors to be aware of this fact as it means that the option tracks the underlying stock less and less as time passes by.

The delta of an option is a very useful property to consider when deciding which option series to choose.

The following worked example will help illustrate this point.

Suppose that the market price of a share is 200p and an investor expects a moderate, gradual increase in the underlying share's price to around 207p. This would represent a seven point rise in the underlying. The table below lays out the assumptions used in this example.

Series	Price	Delta
180p call option (in-the-money)	22p	0.75
220p call option (out-the-money)	1.8p	0.19

The seven point move in the underlying will be mirrored by a corresponding 5.25 (0.75 x 7) increase in the 180p call option, resulting in a 23.86% increase in the 180p call option. The 220p call option similarly increases by 1.33 (0.19 x 7), resulting in a 73.8% increase. From the above calculation, it can be seen that, in percentage terms, the 220p call option would be a better investment.

The calculation of the expected option appreciation (or return on investment) is as follows:

$$\text{Option appreciation (\%)} = \frac{D x I \times 100\%}{P}$$

Where:

D is defined as the number part (ignoring the sign) of the delta of the option.

I is defined as the increase in points in the underlying share – (seven in the above example).

P is defined as the purchase price of the option.

(Note : transaction costs have been omitted for simplicity)

A combined position (ie. a combination of calls and puts) also has a net delta value (known as the position delta) which gives a measure of the risk of the (combined) position, ie. the amount by which the value of the combined position will change for a given point change in the price of the underlying.

This net delta position (or more correctly position delta) is calculated as the sum of the deltas of the options constituting the position. A few examples may help explain the calculation.

Example 1:
A position comprises three purchased in-the-money call options each with a delta of 0.75. The delta of the position is calculated as follows: (3 x 0.75) = 2.25.

Example 2:
A position comprises five sold out-the-money put options each with a delta of -0.45. The delta of the position is calculated as follows: (-5) x (- 0.45) = 2.25.

Example 3:
A position comprises three purchased in-the-money call options , each with a delta of 0.75 and five purchased put options each with a delta of -0.45. The delta of the position is calculated as follows: (3 x 0.75) + (5)x(-0.45) = 0.

This is an example of a delta neutral position.

GAMMA

The gamma is the rate at which an option's delta changes as the price of the underlying changes. The gamma is an important measure of risk associated with an option. In general, options with large gammas are risky and should be avoided by inexperienced investors. The gamma of an option is sometimes known as the curvature of the option. At-the-money options have greater gammas than both in-the-money and out-the-money options.

It is important to remember that the delta of an option or a position is not constant, and fluctuates continually as the variables change. Option writers and investors employing certain more sophisticated option strategies would need to offset their positions by establishing a delta-neutral hedge (a position with a net delta of zero). However, since the delta varies with the underlying, such a position does not remain delta neutral and would need constant monitoring to maintain delta neutral. The delta gives a 'snapshot' or instantaneous view of the degree of risk and by how much an option's price will change for every point movement in the underlying at the time it is calculated. However, a snapshot view alone of the position may not be enough and more sophisticated option investors (with more fanciful strategies) may need to have a fuller picture of how the delta of a position will change given a corresponding one point change in the price of the underlying (index level).

This is where the gamma comes in useful. The gamma is a precise measurement of how the delta changes with respect to the changes in the price of the underlying. By keeping the gamma of the position close to zero, the position can be made to be largely insensitive to large changes in the price of the underlying. The gamma can also be useful to the private investor as it indicates how quickly the delta is likely to change given a point change in the underlying. You can think of the

▲

delta as the speed of the option's price and the gamma as the **acceleration** of the option's price. Therefore high gamma values are associated with high risk (or reward). A simple way of calculating the gamma would be to calculate the gradient of a chart of the delta plotted against the price of the underlying – with all other parameters held constant.

A numerical example might further help illustrate use of the gamma.

Suppose you have a stock with a market price of 180p and a call option on the stock has a delta of 0.30 and a gamma of 0.05. If the stock moves up by 10 points to 190p, the delta of the call option will increase by 5% of the stock move, ie. 0.05 x 10 = 0.5, thus the delta will increase from 0.3 to 0.8. It is important to note that the gamma is not a constant since, if it were, the maximum value of 1 for the delta will be exceeded. As the stock price moves away from the strike price in either direction, the gamma decreases, reducing to its minimum value of zero. The gamma of an option has its maximum value when the price of the stock is close to the exercise price of the option. It can also be seen that the deeply in-the-money or deeply out-the-money options have gammas close to zero – thus the delta of deep in-the-money or deep out-the-money options does not change very much.

As the time to expiry approaches the gamma of at-the-money options increases dramatically. Generally, short-dated options have very low gammas deeply in- or out-the-money, but have the highest gamma when at-the-money. The gamma is also dependent on the volatility of the underlying and at-the-money options on less volatile stocks have larger gammas than options on more volatile securities. For low volatility shares, the at-the-money options have larger gammas than the other higher volatility counterparts. However, as the exercise price increases, the gammas for the more volatile options increase until the more volatile options have higher gammas than those with lower volatility.

Long option positions, whether puts or calls, have positive gamma, whereas short options have negative gamma. The gamma of a position can be calculated and this calculated position gamma shows how the position delta will change for a point change in the price of the underlying share.

VEGA

This characteristic is a measure of an option's sensitivity to volatility. The vega of an option is the change in theoretical value for each one percentage point change in volatility and can be thought of as an indicator of how far the option's price is sensitive to the volatility of the underlying. Both puts and calls have positive vega values – since increasing volatilities are accompanied by increasing premiums (option values).

The vega is always expressed as a positive number. The reason is that option prices are positively correlated to the volatility of the underlying stock. An increase in volatility of the underlying stock results in an increase in option premiums. Similarly, a decrease in volatility of the underlying stock results in a decrease of option premiums. The vega is therefore a risk measure which indicates how quickly the price of the option 'flutters around' as the volatility of the underlying stock changes. A numerical example follows to further illustrate use of the vega.

Assume a share trades in the market for 220p, and the September 250 call is trading for 47p. Given that the vega of the option is 0.25 and the current volatility of the underlying share is 0.30 (30%), we would like to know how much the option premium will be affected by changes in the volatility of the underlying stock. If the stock's volatility increased by 1 point (1%), the value of the option will increase by 0.25 points to 47.25p. If the volatility fell by 1% instead, the option would fall by 0.25 points to 46.75.

THETA

This characteristic is also known as the time decay factor. It is usually expressed as points lost per day. Large positive values of gamma are associated with large negative values of theta and thus every position is a trade-off between market movement and time decay. The theta is a risk measure that indicates option sensitivity to time, ie. the rate at which an option's premium changes (decays) relative to the time left in the option. It is important that option investors are aware that time works in favour of option writers and against option buyers because an option is a decaying asset. The theta of very long-term options is close to zero. Conversely, the theta of short-term options is quite high and tends to have the highest values when the options are at-the-money. Option series with higher implied volatility generally have a higher theta than other series on the same underlying share.

RHO

This is the sensitivity of an option to a change in interest rates. For equity options, interest rates have the least impact on option prices and are thus largely ignored by most equity and index option traders.

Using the greeks, it is possible for the advanced option trader to construct elaborate option strategies, but such strategies are beyond the scope of this book. The more adventurous option investor who has a good understanding of the greeks will find several strategies available to him/her and may even discover a new, unique or 'personalised' strategy that takes advantage of the behaviour of options as described by the 'greeks'.

Summary

Options should not be selected solely on a basis of their deltas, other factors such as the gamma and the volatility of the underlying stock should be taken into consideration.

Here are a few guidelines for option selection:

- Generally, avoid at-the-money options.

- Generally, avoid options with a high gamma.

- Generally, select series with high deltas.

- Generally, buy options which are underpriced, sell overpriced options.

- Generally, buy options, when the volatility of the underlying is lower than its historic 'norm' or average, and sell options when the volatility of the underlying is higher than its historic 'norm' or average. This is because volatility exhibits a property known as 'mean reversion' which means that volatility tends to revert back towards its average value. As you may recall, an increase in volatility causes options to become more expensive.

* * *

Chapter 4
CALCULATING THE VOLATILITY OF OPTIONS

Volatility is of paramount importance to option traders. The volatility of a share is a measure of the amount of variation in returns on the share – a highly volatile share could appreciate rapidly with little or no prior warning (resulting in high rates of return for the investor) – but could equally fall rapidly with little or no notice. It goes without saying that the more volatile a stock is, the greater the associated risk – and consequently, option writers will demand greater 'compensation' for assuming more risk. This explains why options premiums increase with the volatility of the underlying.

The volatility of the underlying (FT-SE 100 index in the case of index options) also happens to be the most important parameter fed into the pricing model being used to evaluate an option – ie. the price of an option depends on the volatility of the underlying. Most of the parameters used in valuing options are readily available and there is not much uncertainty about their values. For example, the level of the index is not debatable. Similarly, the strike price and expiry date do not change and are not disputable. Volatility is the greatest cause of discrepancy in option valuations. To see why, we must first take a closer look at volatility, and try to give an unambiguous definition of it.

There are four types of volatility, namely:

1. *Historical volatility.*

2. *Future volatility.*

3. *Forecast volatility.*

4. *Implied volatility.*

Historical volatility, as the name suggests, is estimated from historical prices. I shall not delve too deeply into the exact mathematics of the calculation, though it is sufficient to point out that historical volatility is estimated by calculating the standard deviation of the closing prices over a period. The (perhaps obvious) problem with this method is that the calculated historical volatility is dependent on the period used in the calculation. This is what gives rise to discrepancies for annualised volatilities. Historical volatility calculated using daily data will be different from historical volatility estimated using weekly (five day) data. Generally, the shorter the time interval used for the volatility estimation calculation, the better is the estimate obtained, since more information goes into the calculation. Weekly estimates (using prices separated by 5 trading days) are therefore, superior to monthly estimates (using prices separated by 20 trading days). Using daily estimates (prices separated by one day) is generally the most commonly used method.

Future volatility is what every option trader would like to know: the volatility that the underlying would exhibit in the future. If a trader could know the future volatility, then he/she would know the future distribution of prices – ie. he/she would know the right 'odds'. In the long run (in a statistical sense) such a trader would expect to make a large number of winning trades (certainly more than would be suggested by a 'fair' game). Option traders do not concern themselves too much with trying to determine future volatility – since at the moment, there are no known reliable ways of accurately predicting it. Future volatility is therefore of little practical importance and is only included for completeness. Using historical volatility as an estimate of the volatility of the underlying, though not totally accurate, is the best proxy for future volatility that option traders have at present. An underlying which has been notoriously volatile in the past is not likely to suddenly become 'well behaved' and acquire stability (ie. low volatility) for a sustained measure of time, or vice-versa. In fact, the very fact that an underlying has departed from its normal volatility pattern offers more sophisticated option investors the opportunity to speculate, in effect betting that the volatility of the underlying will return to normal.

It is assumed that in the absence of external factors – ie. 'price shocks' – the behaviour of the price of an underlying is fairly stable and therefore historical volatility normally provides a good indication as to the likely behaviour of the price in the future. To further explain the concept of historical volatility, we will now manually calculate the volatilities of the FT-SE 100 index and one of its constituents (British Aerospace) over the space of two trading weeks or 10 days. The values used in the table on page 88 are those for the level of the FT-SE 100 index and share price of British Aerospace over 10 consecutive days falling between late February and early March 1996. The calculated historical volatility estimate will be known as 10 day (or two week) historical volatility since it is calculated over 10 days. It is important to remember that a week in trading is five rather than seven days. The obtained values must be annualised before any meaningful comparisons can be made between two volatilities calculated over different time periods. Option pricing models also require the annualised volatility estimate rather than the raw calculated number. Henceforth, any further mention of historical volatility will refer to the annualised historical volatility unless explicitly stated otherwise.

	Level of FT-SE 100	Share price of British Aerospace
Day 1	3714.6	842
Day 2	3725.6	843
Day 3	3740.0	852
Day 4	3740.3	865
Day 5	3704.3	865
Day 6	3715.9	875
Day 7	3738.2	869
Day 8	3727.6	870
Day 9	3752.7	891
Day 10	3768.6	886
Annualised 10 day historical volatility :	8.30%	16.52%

As you will have noticed, the prices used are those that have occurred in the past, ie. they are historical. That is why volatility obtained using this type of calculation is known as historical volatility. We shall use a quick method of calculating the volatility, using the well known formula for standard deviation.

VOLATILITY: A measure of the degree at which the price of the underlying tends to fluctuate.

Standard Deviation Formula for calculating historical volatility:

$$\sum_{i=1}^{N} \frac{(Pi - \bar{P})^2}{N - 1}$$

Where:
Pi is the current price.
$\bar{P}$ is the mean of the prices over a period of N days.

From the table, it can be observed that the annualised historical volatility of British Aerospace (a FT-SE 100 constituent) is significantly higher than the annualised historical volatility of the FT-SE 100 index over the same period.

Historical volatility can be expressed either as a decimal (eg. 0.28) or as a percentage (28%) and its value rarely exceeds 1.0 (or 100%). If an index has a 20 day historical volatility of 5% (or 0.05), then roughly speaking, you would expect the level of the index to remain within 5% of its current level, over the next 20 days.

Volatility is of paramount importance when determining the price of an option.

A more accurate formula for calculating the historical volatility involves the not too friendly looking formula, shown below.

The formula for the calculation of historical volatility (as used by the Option Evaluator™)

$$\sum_{i=1}^{N} \frac{(Xi - \bar{X})^2}{(N-1)}$$

Where:

$$Xi = \ln\left(\left|\frac{Pi}{Pi-1}\right|\right)$$

$$\bar{X} = \frac{1}{N} \sum_{i=1}^{N} Xi$$

ln (X) is the natural logarithm, or $\log_e(X)$

$\left|\ \ \right|$ is the modulus operator, or 'positive part' of the expression

Pi   is the current price

Pi - ₁   s the previous day's price

and N is the number of days.

Incidentally, it is worth noting at this point that it is not necessary to manually calculate historical volatilities or even know how they are calculated. Your broker (if you have one) may have access to **annualised** historical volatility over several time periods, typically 5 day, 10 day, 20 day, 60 day and 120 day volatilities. If you do not have a broker (or your broker cannot provide you with historical volatility estimates), don't despair, all is not lost! You will be pleased to know that the accompanying software, *Option Evaluator™*, allows you to calculate the annualised volatilities of an underlying (share, index etc.) by typing in the prices of the underlying. Further information on how to do this is provided in the accompanying help file under **Advanced Features**.

The dependence of historical volatility on the time used in the calculation explains why it is important that investors use a period similar or equal to the proposed period of investment. In other words, you don't just arbitrarily pick a period over which the historical volatility is calculated. As stated earlier, the time period over which the historical volatility is calculated has an influence on the value of the historical volatility estimate obtained. Additionally, it means that if you intend to hold an option for one month for example, then the sort of historical volatility you should be interested in is the one month or 20 day annualised historical volatility estimate.

Another useful feature of volatility is that it allows us to predict the likely values of the price of the underlying in the future. I use the word 'predict' rather reluctantly as the values obtained by the method to be described shortly are more of an estimate based on statistical assumptions. The degree of confidence we attach to this estimate is known as a **confidence interval**. For example, if we double the volatility and add this value to the current level of the index, we obtain a new level that will give the highest level the index will obtain in the future (under certain statistical assumptions). Similarly, if we subtract twice the standard deviation from the current price of the underlying, we obtain the lowest level the index is likely to achieve in the future. The confidence interval associated with this calculation is 95%. In other words, there is a 95% probability that the level of the index will lie somewhere between the highest and the lowest value calculated. Similarly, by multiplying the standard deviation by three (instead of two as before) we obtain a *high* and a *low* value again, but this time with a wider confidence level of 99%. Roughly translated, there is a 99% probability that the index will lie somewhere between the new *high* and the *low* value calculated.

The following numeric example will demonstrate this:

Assume that at a certain point in time, the FT-SE 100 index has an annualised 20 day historical volatility estimate of 0.065 (or 6.5%). Further assume that the current level of the index is 3800. We can calculate the expected level of the FT-SE 100 index over the next 20 days as follows:

Using a 95% confidence interval

For a 95% confidence interval, we will multiply the historical volatility by a factor of two. The new figure obtained is 13.0%. Now, 13.0% of the level of the index (3800) = 494.

So we can say that there is a 95% probability that the index will remain between the 3306 and 4294 levels over the next 20 days (the historical volatility estimate was based on 20 days).

Lowest likely value in the next 20 days	Highest likely value in the next 20 days
= (3800 − 494) = 3306	= (3800 + 494) = 4294

Using a 99% confidence interval

For a 99% confidence interval, we will multiply the historical volatility by a factor of three. The new figure obtained is 19.5%. Now, 19.5 % of the level of the index (3800) = 741.

So we can say that there is a 99% probability that the index will remain between the 3059 and 4541 levels over the next 20 days.

Please note that this method of calculation depends on very strong statistical assumptions of independence and normality of the values of the level of the index which in practice may not be satisfied. It is therefore, only a 'rough and ready' rule and must not be relied on as being an accurate indicator of the distribution of future levels of the index.

Lowest likely value **in the next 20 days**	**Highest likely value** **in the next 20 days**
= (3800 − 741) = 3059	= (3800 + 741) = 4541

Forecast volatility is an estimate or forecast of future volatility which is offered as a service by certain research firms. It is still in its infancy, and must be considered an inexact science at best. However, an option trader's guess of the future volatility of the underlying may very well take into consideration any volatility forecasts to which he/she may have access.

Implied volatility and historic volatility are the most important types of volatility as far as the practical option investor is concerned. Since volatility is such an important factor in determining the price of an option, option traders often 'invert' the pricing formulae to try to determine the volatility of the underlying (index in our case), given that the price of the option is known. By 'inverting' the pricing formulae, I mean that option traders often feed the market price of an option along with the exercise price and expiry date into a pricing model and get the software to work 'backwards' to find out what volatility of the underlying is being *implied* by the option's price. This kind of volatility is known as **implied volatility** and is of considerable interest to the professional option trader since this is the volatility being *implied* by the market price of the option. Professional option investors spend a lot of time studying and constructing option strategies that can take advantage of options whose implied volatility is too high (or too low) compared with historical standards.

The following scenario might help to explain the concept of implied volatility further. Assume that an option trader has access to 'correct' data (ie. index level, exercise price) as inputs to a pricing model, further assume that all other market participants (including market-makers) use the same pricing model – say the Black-Scholes for evaluating options (this is a strong assumption given that by far the most popular option pricing models are the Black-Scholes and Binomial for European and American options respectively). The option trader in our example could well find that the market has 'mis-priced' the option, ie. the option is selling in the market at a different value from its theoretical or 'fair value', but from our initial assumption, the inputs are 'correct' – so why the price differential? This apparent inaccuracy is caused by the volatility estimate used in the model. The market in this case is implying a different volatility for the option. It is this value of volatility that, when fed into the pricing model, will result in the market price of the option. Generally, option traders like to buy options that have a lower implied volatility than the historical volatility **average** as the volatility is expected to increase again back to its normal value, thereby increasing the value of the option – which can then be sold at a profit. When this occurs, professional option traders say that implied volatility is *trading at a discount* (to historical volatility). Similarly, option traders generally tend to sell option series that have an implied volatility much higher than the historical volatility average, as the volatility of the underlying is expected to drop downward toward the average, allowing the option to be bought back at a lower price and thus realising a profit.

Please note that for the purpose of illustration of the importance of implied volatility in formulating strategies, I have grossly over-simplified or ignored the other factors that should be taken into account when implementing such strategies. Option traders should not attempt these kinds of sophisticated trades if they are not sure of what they are doing.

As we discovered in earlier chapters, indices generally have a lower volatility than their constituent shares. This is partly due to the fact that the gains in the price of the shares of certain constituent companies will be offset (or at least partly mitigated) by corresponding losses on the value of the shares of other constituent companies and partly due to the fact that the constituent companies are more vulnerable to 'price shocks' such as the resignation of a company director, a profits warning or being the subject of a take-over bid. This generally makes individual companies riskier than the entire market. The corresponding relative low volatility of the FT-SE 100 is translated into generally cheaper option prices when compared to equity options.

Once again, I should remind you that I have made several simplifications in this chapter to make the concept of volatility accessible to a wider reading audience, and some of the calculations made (for example, the one for forecasting levels of the index) should be used as a general rule of thumb rather than followed as a mantra or a magic formula.

* * *

Chapter 5
USING THE OPTION EVALUATOR™

Analysing options can involve several calculations which would be far too laborious and time consuming if attempted manually. The existence of new option analysis software programs such as the one included with this book dramatically cuts down the time needed to evaluate options and also reduces the level of mathematical understanding required to make the necessary calculations. In many cases it is simply a case of supplying the appropriate variables and clicking a button to calculate the required values.

Investors must be aware of the limitations of models. A 'model' is defined in the Chambers Dictionary as 'an imitation of something on a smaller scale'. Models are constructed to help understand better the entity being modelled. A model may be very similar to what it models, but the model is unlikely to duplicate every feature of the real world. It is therefore unwise to assume that the model and the real world which it represents are identical in every way. The astute investor will make use of pricing models, but with full awareness of what they can and cannot do. For example there is no way that all future price shocks (by definition unpredictable) such as the assassination of a president, or 'acts of God' such as adverse weather conditions, can be factored into a model.

▲

All models are based on assumptions, which may or may not be strong, statistically speaking. Additionally, a model's output is only as good as the input data with which it is fed – remember: garbage in, garbage out. There is no point having the best pricing models in the world if you enter incorrect values of volatilities (say) – the pricing model is likely to yield 'unexpected' results. As we saw in the previous chapter, future volatility (or perceptions of the future volatility of the underlying), though one of the most important determinants of an option's price, remains elusive and we have to make do with historical volatility estimates instead. Since historical volatility estimates are the best indicator we have of the future volatility of the underlying option, investors should endeavour to obtain the most reliable estimates of historical volatility possible. It is of paramount importance that the historical volatility estimate used in pricing an option has the same period – that is, the volatility should be calculated over the same length of time as your intended investment horizon. In other words, if you expect to hold an option for its remaining life (one month, say), obtain the annualised estimate of one month's historical volatility of the underlying.

Those with a machismo streak may choose to calculate manually the historical volatility for one month by using the formula for standard deviation described earlier on. However, for mere mortals, it is much simpler, quicker and less prone to error to use the software provided to calculate annualised historical volatility estimates (the software uses the more complicated, but more accurate, formula given on page 90). This can be achieved by clicking on the 'Advanced' button in Option Evaluator™. Assuming an investment horizon of one month (ie. 20 days), enter the last 20 closing prices in the field provided and then click on the 'Calculate' button. The displayed calculated output is the annualised one month (or 20 day) volatility of the underlying. This value can then be used in the main input screen to evaluate an option based on the underlying.

A novice option trader may be likened to an individual entering a dark room for the first time. The option trader who is armed with some basic understanding of pricing models and how to use them enters the same room – but with a small candle. The trader with the small candle is more likely to find what he/she is looking for (profits) than the investor with no light source. Successful option traders find pricing models an invaluable tool in selecting options and implementing strategies. However, to make the best use of pricing models, traders must be aware of their limitations as well as their strengths. Just as the flickering light of a candle may cause you to see shadows of things that are not really there, an over-zealous interpretation of calculated values can lead to errors. Like the individual finding his/her way in a dark room with the aid of a candle as a light source, with experience comes better judgement and the investor is able to tell the 'shadows' apart from the 'real objects' (profits) being sought.

The software package included

This book is accompanied by a 30 use* demonstration version of the Option Evaluator™ – a powerful yet simple to use option analysis program. It provides a set of option and future evaluation functions which brings to Windows users powerful analysis tools normally only available to market professionals. Before the advent of option analysis software packages, most investors approached options trading just like gambling. They placed trades without analysing them and without knowing their chances for success. The Option Evaluator™ is incredibly easy to use and is designed for all option traders – from beginner to experienced professional. No prior detailed knowledge of options is assumed, although a basic

*Note: 30 use applies to the fact that the demonstration software can be run for a maximum number of thirty times. The software is available by contracting the author. (see back of this book for details). Alternatively, you may contact Market Data Centre   Ltd on Tel: 0171 522 0094 or Fax 0171 522 0095

▲

understanding of options is required to be able fully to use this software to its maximum potential. The software has been written with the private investor in mind but it is also flexible, powerful and reliable enough to be used by market professionals. It will also be possible to use a real-time data feed with a later version of the software. The mathematical pricing models available with this package are the Black-Scholes and its various derivations (Black and Garman-Kohlhagen) for European style options, and the Binomial (Cox-Ross-Rubinstein) for American style options. An on-line glossary of options terminology is provided, as well as several pages detailing the standard derivative contracts traded on LIFFE.

FEATURES OF THE
OPTION EVALUATOR™ VERSION 1.5

1. Enables users to calculate the theoretical (fair value) for both American style and European style options and also allows for the evaluation of options derived from the following:
    i.   Equity.
    ii. Index.
    iii. Currency.
    iv. Commodity.
    v.   Future.
    vi. Bond.
    vii. OTC options.

2. Enables users to calculate the various option sensitivities:
    i.   Delta.
    ii. Gamma.
    iii. Theta.
    iv. Vega.

     v. Eta (Elasticity).
     vi. Domestic Rho.
     vii. Foreign Rho (Currency options only).

3. Enables users to calculate the implied volatility for a selected option series.

4. Allows users to forecast various outcomes including:
   i.   Probability of the selected option position making a profit.
   ii. Probability of the option expiring in-the-money.
   iii. Expected value of the underlying at expiry.
   iv. Expected profit at expiry.

5. Allows users to calculate the fair value of futures and forward contracts (useful for arbitrage trades, or determining when program trades are likely to 'kick-in').

6. Allows users to calculate their own estimates of historical volatility.

7. Automatically calculates the expiry dates for LIFFE traded equity and index options and options based on futures (making an exchange calendar redundant).

8. Enables users to save their calculations (worksheets) and reload them at a later time. Worksheets can be given descriptive titles to identify the option being evaluated. The title (if available) appears on all printed reports and charts.

9. Enables users to calculate an option's percentage deviation from its theoretical or fair value (ie. by how much an option is overpriced or underpriced).

10. Features an on-line help and glossary of option terminology – making it an invaluable tool for complete beginners and experienced option traders alike. It also provides comprehensive contract specifications on ALL standard LIFFE traded derivatives.

11. Features a charting facility, enabling users to view profit/loss diagrams on their positions. The Profit/Loss Chart also displays vital statistics such as the break-even probability etc. The Profit Chart may also be printed.

12. Features an in-built report generator for printing a complete analytical breakdown report of the option being evaluated.

Hardware and software requirements

Software requirements
Microsoft Windows 3.1 (or later). It also runs on Windows 95 and Windows NT.

Hardware requirements
The Option Evaluator™ will run on any PC capable of running Windows 3.1 (or later). However, evaluating options involves numerous complex mathematical routines using floating point number precision for accuracy. The software will therefore run much faster on a 486 DX or a Pentium PC. The software automatically seeks a maths co-processor when running, and will execute all mathematical routines on a co-processor (if one is present). Certain calculations which, by their nature, place great demand on the processor (eg. implied volatility calculations on an American style option) may be noticeably slower on less powerful machines.
The program also requires a pointing device or a mouse.

Installing the application

Note: The following instructions assume that your 3.5" floppy drive is configured as the 'A' drive. Please type in 'B' in place of 'A', if your 3.5" floppy drive is configured as your 'B' drive.

To install the Option Evaluator™ version 1.5 :

1. *Place the installation diskette provided in your floppy drive.*

2. *Choose File Run from Program Manager (or Run from the Start button for Windows 95) and type A:\SETUP.*

3. *When prompted for the location of the set-up files (by the set-up program), click on the CONTINUE button to continue. (Note that you must type in B:\ at this prompt before continuing if your 3.5" floppy drive is configured as your 'B' drive.)*

4. *Accept the default (C:\EVALCALC) then click on the CONTINUE button.*

5. *The set-up process should then proceed to compress the necessary files, create the Program Manager group 'Option Evaluator™ Version 1.5 and group icons and then inform you when the set-up is completed successfully.*

To run the Option Evaluator™ software, double click on the bulb icon in the newly created 'Option Evaluator™' group.

Using the Option Evaluator™ (getting started)

When using the Option Evaluator™, enter the various required inputs in the provided fields. If invalid data is entered in a field, you are prompted with a message box that tells you what is wrong when you attempt to perform a calculation. When all the fields (Underlying, Exercise price etc.) are correctly entered – simply click on the Calculate button. The various outputs are then automatically calculated and displayed in the Calculated Outputs frame. You can then copy a calculated result and paste it into any other Windows application (by double clicking on the required field and selecting copy from the edit menu). An on-line help system is available to point you to relevant information should you require further information.

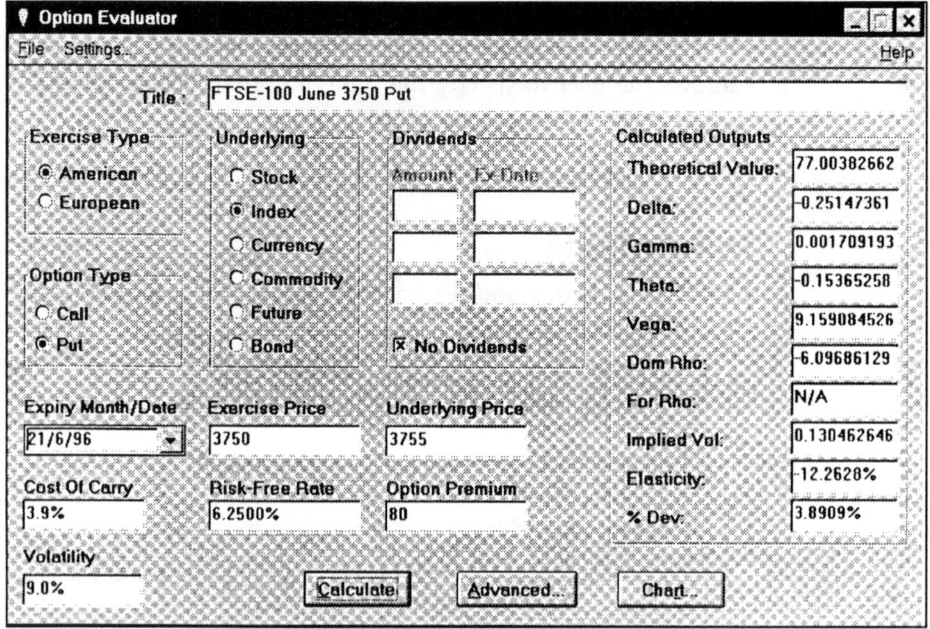

Option Evaluator™ – main calculation screen

The figure above depicts the main calculation screen of the Option Evaluator™, which requires you to enter certain details before a calculation can be made. Even though some of the input parameters are self explanatory, we shall consider each of them in turn.

Exercise type

Selecting one of the two radio buttons available in this group allows the user to specify the exercise type of the option – ie. either European or American (see glossary on page 163).

Option type

Selecting one of the two radio buttons available in this group allows the user to specify the type of option to be evaluated – allows either a call or put.

Underlying

Select the corresponding underlying instrument from which your option is derived – for example to evaluate stock options, select stock or to evaluate the FT-SE 100, S&P 100 (or any other index), select index as the underlying – and so on.

Underlying Price

This is the price at which the underlying (eg. shares for a stock option evaluation) is trading in the market. Always use the offer price, since this is the price you would have to pay to buy the underlying in the market. For example, if you wanted to evaluate options on the April 3750 FT-SE 100 index calls and the index was at 3780 you would select index as the underlying, and enter 3780 in the underlying price text box. In the case of share option valuations, select stock as the underlying, and enter the level of the index in the underlying price text box.

Dividend

These input fields allow you to enter future dividend streams (up to three dividend receipts falling within the life of the option) to be incorporated in pricing the option. They are automatically set to zero (ie. the underlying is assumed not to pay any dividends during the life of the option) when the application first starts. If there are no dividends to be received then leave the settings as they are. These fields are only available for equity (share) options and are automatically made inactive when the underlying instrument is not a stock. It is imperative that you use the same price units for all price fields (Dividends, Option Premium, Underlying Price, Exercise Price etc.) otherwise the model will produce erroneous results. The continuous dividend yield model is used in evaluating index options. To include the effect of dividends on index options, enter the dividend yield on the index in the cost of carry field (see page 111). Discrete dividend modelling of index options is not supported in this version of the program.

Ex-dividend date

These input fields allow you to enter the ex-dividend dates (for up to three future dividends to be received within the life of the option) to be incorporated in pricing the option. If only one dividend is to be received, just fill the first pair (dividend amount and ex-dividend date) and leave the other two pairs blank.

No dividend check box

If there are no dividends receivable during the life of the option, check this box. The dividend and ex-dividend field boxes become inactive (greyed out) and any values originally entered are ignored.

Expiry month

Simply select the month in which the contract expires and the expiry date is automatically calculated based on the current month (for equity options, index options and options on futures – no need for an exchange calendar!) – the calculated dates are correct for LIFFE (London International Financial Futures and Options Exchange) equity and index products and users may need to enter manually expiry dates for options traded on other exchanges. Users will also have to enter manually their preferred expiry date when evaluating commodity options, bond options, OTC (Over the Counter) or LIFFE FLEX options. The default expiry month (when the Option Evaluator™ is first run) is the current month; if the expiry date for the current month and the chosen underlying instrument (stock) has already gone by, the expiry date of the next month is selected.

Option premium

This is the market price (offer price) of the option to be evaluated. It is required when implied volatility, or the percentage deviation from fair value, is required as the output – and is ignored otherwise. It is important that the same price units are used when entering prices. Profit/loss charts cannot be displayed unless the option premium has been entered. Several statistics in the Advanced section also depend on the option premium being entered.

Exercise price

This is the exercise (see Glossary on page 163) or strike price of the option to be evaluated. It is important that the same price units are used when entering prices.

Risk free rate

This is the interest rate available on 'riskless' investments such as treasury bills – for simplicity (and as a useful approximation), domestic interest rates can be entered in this field. Interest rates can be entered as percentages (eg. 6.25%) or as the equivalent number (0.0625 in this case). If you enter an interest rate as a percentage, you must include the % character, otherwise the value is interpreted as a literal number – resulting in a wrongly calculated output. A tip is to set your interest rate in the settings dialogue box – this allows the software automatically to insert your default interest rate in this field every time you evaluate a new option.

Cost of carry

This is a measure of the storage cost plus the interest that is paid to finance the asset, less any income earned on the asset. Option Evaluator™ automatically enters values in this field for you and in most cases it must be left alone. When evaluating options on dividend paying stocks or coupon bearing bonds, you have two choices:

1. *Use discrete dividend modelling by entering the cash dividends or coupon payments and the day on which they fall (or the date on which the underlying stock goes ex-dividend in the case of stocks) and leaving the cost of carry field with the value automatically entered by Option Evaluator™ . This is the simplest and quickest way of valuing options on dividend paying stocks. If no dividends are receivable within the life of an option on a dividend paying stock, for greater accuracy, you may use the continuous yield model described below.*

2. *Use continuous yield modelling by entering the annualised yield on the stock or bond in the cost of carry field.*

The cost of carry for options derived from different underlyings are as follows:

1. *For a non-dividend paying stock, the value to be entered in the cost of carry field is the interest rate (automatically entered for you in the cost of carry field) since there are no storage charges and no income is earned.*

2. *For options on dividend paying stocks, indices, coupon bearing bonds etc., use either discrete dividend modelling (simplest) or continuous yield modelling as described above. Note that the two models provided are mutually exclusive – ie. you should not enter dividends receivable and change the value in the cost of carry field as well.*

3. *For options on a commodity held solely for investment (eg. gold and silver), the value to be entered in the cost of carry field is the annualised storage cost expressed as a percentage of the price of the commodity. This annualised percentage must be entered as a negative number since this is equivalent to a negative dividend yield.*

4. *For options on futures, the value to be entered in the cost of carry is zero (automatically entered for you when the selected underlying is a future).*

5. *For currency options, the value to be entered in the cost of carry field is the foreign interest rate.*

The cost of carry can be entered as percentages (eg. 2.75%) or as the equivalent number (0.0275 in this case). If you enter the cost of carry as a percentage, you must follow the number with the percentage (%) character, otherwise the value is interpreted as a literal number – resulting in a wrongly calculated output.

Volatility

This is the annualised historical volatility of the underlying. Annualised historical volatility estimates can be obtained from various sources. However, an estimate is obtainable using the Historical Volatility Estimate command under the Advanced Features. This value can then be used in the main form to evaluate an option on the underlying. Volatility can be entered as a percentage (eg. 18.75%) or as the equivalent number (0.1875 in this case). If you enter volatility as a percentage, you must include the % character, otherwise the value is interpreted as a literal number – resulting in a wrongly calculated output.

Calculate button

When this button is pressed, values are automatically calculated and displayed in the Calculated Outputs field.

> *Tip* : When evaluating options, remember to use the same units for all the price inputs – ie. do not enter certain price inputs in pounds sterling (for example) and others in pence. Always remember to omit the currency symbols (£,$,p etc.) and enter only the numeric values.

A tip is to work in pennies rather than pounds – ie. enter 502 (for example) instead of £5.02 – since working with small numbers may lead to imprecision due to rounding-off errors when evaluating certain parameters.

Let's now take a quick look at the outputs available – the calculated outputs.

Theoretical value

This field is the theoretical value or fair value of the option being analysed – using the user-entered data for historical volatility, exercise price, underlying price, expiry date, interest rate etc. The theoretical values generated by the program are the offer prices (ie. the price at which you should be able to purchase the option in the market). The Option Evaluator™ uses the Binomial (Cox-Rubinstein) pricing model for determining the theoretical value of American style options and the Black-Scholes pricing model is used for determining the theoretical value of European style options.

The next five values are the automatically calculated values of the greeks, based on the values (exercise price, volatility, expiry date etc.) you have entered into the program. The interpretation of the values of each of these greeks was discussed in Chapter Three.

DELTA

This field displays the delta of the option being calculated.

GAMMA

This field displays the gamma of the option being calculated.

THETA

This field displays the theta of the option being calculated.

VEGA

This field displays the vega of the option being calculated.

DOMESTIC RHO

This field displays the rho of the option being calculated.

FOREIGN RHO

This field displays the foreign rho of the option being calculated. This field will always display 'N/A' unless a currency option is being evaluated.

Implied volatility

This is the implied volatility of the selected option. This calculation is particularly demanding on processors when the implied volatility of an American style option is being found. The software uses a Newton-Raphson search algorithm in determining a value for the implied volatility. Users running this application on a 386 may find it quicker to select a European model when calculating implied volatility since this is calculated much more quickly than for the American model – and the difference in values is not significant. Users running the software on a 486 or Pentium PC will not discern a difference in calculations between an American and European option (ie. they are both instantaneous). Occasionally, due to the values entered as parameters for the pricing model, such as expiry date, exercise price (especially market premium), it is impossible to calculate a value for volatility which satisfies the pricing equation. In these instances the Calculated Output field displays Indeterminate Value. If no option premium has been entered, the implied volatility cannot be calculated and this field will display N/A when the calculate button is clicked.

Note: Interpretation of the values obtained for the implied volatility of an option series was discussed in Chapter Four.

Elasticity

This is the elasticity of the option being calculated. The elasticity (also known as the Eta) is a sensitivity measure that is not as well known as the other greeks and provides a measure of an option's sensitivity to percentage changes in the underlying. That is, the elasticity is the percentage change in the option price with respect to a percentage change in the price of the underlying. It is therefore a measure of the gearing available with the particular option being evaluated. The higher the elasticity of the option series being analysed, the higher the gearing available with the option.

% Dev

This is the % deviation from the theoretical or fair price of the option series being evaluated. The option premium (market price of the option being analysed) is required for this calculation. If the option premium has been omitted, this field will display N/A. Negative values indicate an underpriced option while positive values indicate an over-priced option.

Profit/loss charts

Profit/loss graphs are absolutely essential in illustrating the risk/return profile of a position at expiry and the serious option investor will do well to memorise if not all, at least the basic graphs for simple option strategies such as long call, long put, short call, and short put strategies. The profit/loss graph is constructed by plotting profit on the positive Y axis, loss on the negative Y axis and the price of the underlying on the X axis. For call options, the profit (or loss) is obtained by subtracting the price of the underlying share from the exercise price of the option. Positive values indicate a profit and negative values indicate a loss. For put options, the profit (or loss) is obtained by subtracting the exercise price of the option from the price of the underlying share. Positive values indicate a profit and negative values indicate a loss.

Users of the Option Evaluator™ software package may create profit/loss diagrams for the option being evaluated (and further choose between long and short positions on the option).

A profit/loss chart is displayed (default is a long position) and vital statistics such as break-even probabilities and break-even points are included on the graph. Please note that the Chart button is not available (ie. charts cannot be displayed) if ALL the required inputs have not been entered by the user.

All displayed charts can be printed by clicking the print button on the chart dialogue box.

The chart shown below is an example of a profit/loss chart for a long call option position:

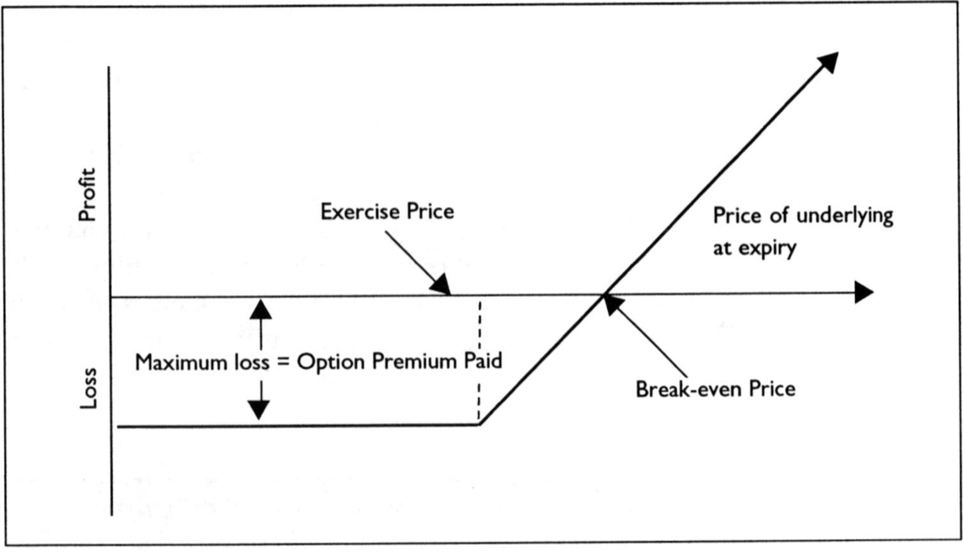

Advanced features

These options become available when the Advanced button is pressed. With the exception of the Historical Volatility Estimate and Fair Value Of Future commands, the Calculate button in the main screen must ALWAYS be pressed BEFORE the Advanced button is pressed – as doing this refreshes the memory with the new values entered. To return to the standard screen, press on the button labelled BACK << (or press the Escape button on your keyboard).

Historical volatility estimate

This feature allows you to estimate the historical volatility of the underlying by entering the closing prices (a minimum of five days' closing prices is required) of the underlying. The annualised historical volatility estimate for the underlying is then calculated – this figure can then be fed into the pricing model (Volatility field). A word of warning however: entering only five days' data (a week's data) is not likely to give you a very useful result especially if there has been a significant change in the price of the underlying in the last five days – this is because you will effectively be using the five day volatility to estimate the annual volatility and your result will be heavily influenced by the five values you have entered. A more useful estimate of historical volatility can be expected when 20 days (one month's data) or more is entered in the closing prices field. Make sure that the closing prices are separated by commas and do not include spaces, zeros or non-numeric characters in the field.

Note: The historical volatility estimate is a very important parameter in determining the price of an option and users must check the validity of the closing prices entered.

Break-even point

This is the price at which an established position (long or short) will break even. This calculation requires the option premium and is more accurate than a simple arithmetic addition of the option premium and the exercise price of the option being evaluated (for long calls or short puts).

Break-even probability

This is the probability that your strategy will break even if held till expiry. It is, in effect, the probability that your position will make a profit (or at least not incur a loss) if held till expiry. You must specify whether your position is long or short (see Glossary on page 163).

ITM at expiry probability

This is the probability of the option expiring in-the-money (see Glossary on page 163). Note: A high ITM probability does not necessarily mean that the position will expire profitable.

Expected terminal price

This is the expected price of the underlying at expiry and is calculated using the same statistical assumptions of *lognormality* of the distribution of changes in the price of the underlying. It is calculated within a 99.994% confidence interval.

Expected terminal profit

This is the expected terminal profit from a long/short option position and is calculated using the same assumptions of lognormality as used in the previous commands – and in various option pricing models.

It may be likely that as a result of several thousand approximations and some truncations (rounding off of floating point numbers) that may be involved in the calculation, that results obtained may not be what is expected. This is most likely to be the case when the series being evaluated are short-dated at-the-money options. The expected terminal profit should be approximately equal to the difference between the expected terminal price and the break-even price. Significant divergence from this figure may suggest that the calculation has been biased by user inputs (see below) or that rounding errors have become significant relative to the calculated result – this becomes most noticeable for at-the-money options as described above.

The Expected Terminal Profit command (like most commands in the Advanced section) is dependent on the values LAST entered on the main form (another cause of unexpected results is forgetting to press the Calculate button before preceding to the Advanced section).

Note: The Expected Terminal Profit command is included as an indicative tool and calculated values should not be interpreted too literally.

* * *

Chapter 6
SOME SIMPLE FINITE
RISK OPTION STRATEGIES

So far in this book we have discussed the academic aspects of options. We have now built enough knowledge to be able to start seriously considering trading in index options. In this chapter, we will start putting the theory into practice and learn about some simple finite risk option strategies.

Before embarking on any investment, it is important to undertake an analysis or appraisal of what you are about to invest in. When using traded options as a speculative medium, timing is of critical importance and therefore technical analysis (which focuses on timing) seems to have a distinct advantage over fundamental analysis when it comes to successful options trading. Needless to say, you must not totally disregard fundamental information when undertaking your preliminary analysis. For example, it will generally be inadvisable to buy call options on the shares of a company that has just issued a profits warning and is closing down several operations – no matter how bullish the technical chart of the share looks. Equally, it would generally be considered unwise to buy put options in a company that has delivered results at the higher end of analysts' forecasts and is likely to be a bid target – no matter how bearish the technical chart of the share appears.

To be a successful options investor you must have fairly good to strong technical analysis skills and must at least be able to draw trendlines. However, you **must** be able to spot and draw support and resistance levels as almost all option strategies are based around support and resistance levels. It is outside the scope of this book to give a detailed discussion on technical analysis. Several good books are available for anyone who may feel he/she needs to polish up on his/her technical analysis skills. I shall assume that you are familiar with basic technical analysis patterns, indicators and some basic Japanese candlestick patterns.

Some simple option strategies

As we have indicated before, because of the gearing available with options, trading in options can be decidedly unhealthy for your bank balance if you do not limit your option strategies to those that are categorised as finite risk (see Glossary on page 163). In this section of the book we shall implement some simple option strategies (all of which are finite risk strategies). More complicated option strategies can be implemented using these strategies.

We will start with the simplest of all finite risk strategies (the long call or long put strategy).

Long call strategy

A long call strategy involves the purchase of a call option. It is a speculative strategy (unless used for anticipatory hedging) that has the added benefit of having a finite risk and unlimited reward (ie. it is a finite risk strategy). This simple option strategy has a very nice reward/risk profile which combines an unlimited maximum profit with a limited risk. The most you can lose in such a strategy is the amount you paid for the call.

Let's take a closer look at the profit/loss graph and try to understand what is really happening. When you first buy the call option, you have established the position for a net debit (since it cost you money), therefore you start off in negative territory. From our earlier discussion on the properties of options, we will want an option with a fairly high delta, so that the price of the option increases at a good rate as the value of the index increases. As the level of the index increases, the loss on the position is gradually offset by the increasing value of the option. As the level of the index increases further, so does the value of the call option until at a certain critical value known as the break-even point, the gain in the value of the option exactly offsets the debit at which the position was established. The break-even point is very important to the option point because after this level, as the index goes higher, the long call option position will start to make a profit.

Mindful of what we've learnt so far, let's now look at how we can tilt the probabilities in our favour as much as possible. The steps to be taken are listed below:

1. *Ideally, the chart of the FT-SE 100 index should be as bullish as possible. Things to look for in the chart include: appearance of a reversal pattern like a head and shoulders bottom, break out of a downtrend via a hammer candlestick and a long white-bodied candle, break out of a bullish flag etc. – all accompanied by good volume. Confirmation by stochastic indicators, moving averages, RSI etc.*

2. *Find out if you can find any fundamental information to back your technical view (ie. bullish news – for the FT-SE 100 index, you may look at the general economy and views on interest rates) – if there is bullish news, then this further increases the probability of your long call position being profitable.*

3. *Establish support and resistance levels on the chart.*

4. *Preferably, the FT-SE 100 index should be bouncing off the support level on good volume.*

5. *Buy calls at a strike price below the support level. By doing so, you dramatically increase the probability of your call expiring in-the-money. You must decide over what period the index is likely to rise (ie. the likely speed of the rise) and buy call options whose life span will be longer than the expected time over which the move will occur. By doing this, you 'buy yourself more time' in case the index doesn't rise as quickly as you had anticipated, therefore decreasing the probability of your option expiring worthless.*

6. *Calculate your break-even point and determine how likely it is for the level of the FT-SE 100 index to increase past the break-even level. The Option Evaluator™ can help you calculate this probability (the break-even probability). Generally, a probability over 45% can be considered favourable.*

7. *Make sure you are not paying 'over the odds'. In other words, make sure that the option is not overpriced; ie. make sure the percentage deviation from the theoretical value is not more than 7% (this is more a rule of thumb than anything else) and must not be adhered to rigidly. Be aware of the prevailing market sentiment.*

8. *Establish a stop-loss (normally set at slightly below the support level). Once this has been breached, ie. once the index closes below this level on heavy volume, the market is telling you that you are wrong. You must then **immediately** liquidate your long call position by selling the previously bought option. This will help you cut your losses on the*

▲

position . The stop-loss must be established before the long call option position is established.

9. *Establish a target level (using technical analysis or whatever form of analysis is available to you). This is the price at which you expect the index to rise (within your investment time horizon).*

10. *Once your established target level has been reached, ie. once the index closes at or above that level, take your profits by selling the calls you had previously bought. Although there are more sophisticated 'follow up' strategies, this is by far the simplest strategy available to novice option traders. In addition, it yields the most consistent results.*

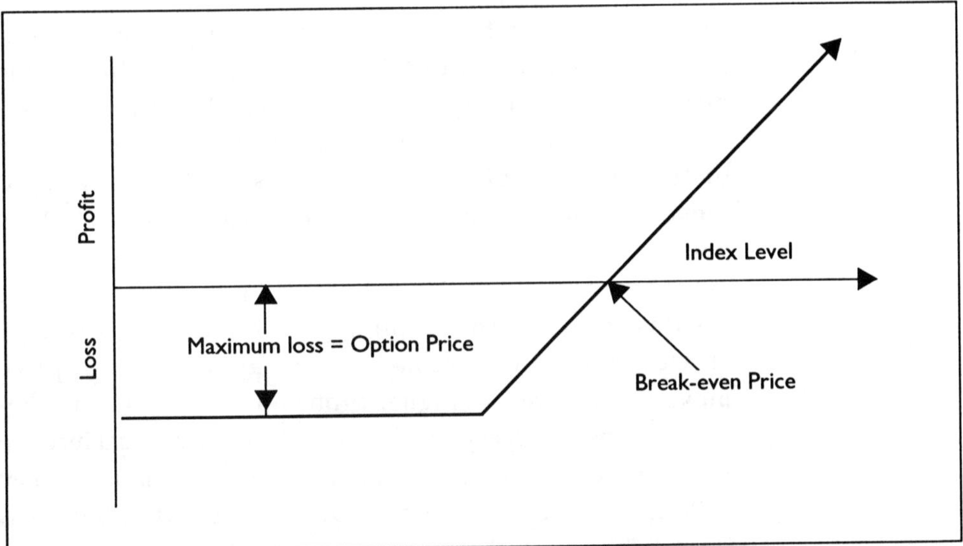

Figure I.

Figure 1 shows a profit/loss graph for a purchased (long) call option, ie. a long call strategy. As can be seen from the graph, this position has limited risk and unlimited return. The option investor must be bullish of the stock to adopt this strategy. This position will incur a finite loss (cost of the option) if the share price falls below the break-even point (cost of the call option plus the exercise price). However, if the stock rises above this break-even point, there is virtually unlimited profit to be achieved. Please note that, for simplicity, we have ignored transaction costs in the construction of these graphs even though it is a fairly simple matter to incorporate them again for greater accuracy. An example of how this may be done is as follows : in Figure 1, the break-even point will be the cost of the call option plus the exercise price, plus any transaction costs (brokerage fees and commission charges etc.).

The effect of timing

Very impressive returns can be achieved implementing this strategy – when you're fairly accurate in predicting the movement of the index and the time interval over which it will occur. The strategy can be adapted to suit the 'aggressiveness' or 'bullishness' of the option investor. If a very rapid movement in the stock price is expected over a short time period (ie. the option investor is very bullish), implementing out-the-money calls in this strategy will generally provide the greatest return – this is an aggressive bullish strategy. However, if you're wrong in your assumption of price movement, there is a higher probability that your out-the-money options will expire worthless. If a more gradual increase in the stock price is expected then implementing in-the-money calls in the strategy will generally be the 'safest bet'. It is important to remember that less aggressive strategies are more likely to achieve a profit (the catch being that the profit realised is always smaller than the profit available using a more aggressive strategy), since rapid stock price movements (especially upwards) are not too common – unless there is a take-over situation (in which case four figure annualised returns are not unheard of). It is generally safer to buy in-the-money calls, where there is less chance of your call option expiring worthless. It is worth noting that by modifying your strategy to suit your degree of aggressiveness, you will be automatically selecting options with the appropriate gamma, theta and vega without even knowing it (at-the-money options tend to have the highest gamma). This is why it is not too important to understand the definitions of these terms. Having said that, it may be obvious to you that if you actually understand what these various greeks mean, you can further fine tune the options you use in your strategy, tilting the probability of a profit.

LONG PUT STRATEGY

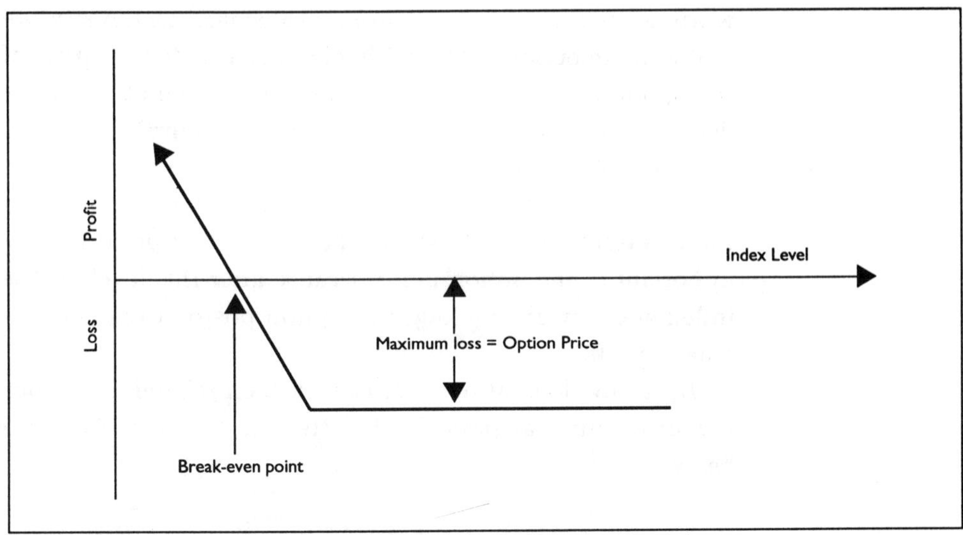

Figure 2.

Much of what has been said for the long call position applies equally in the case of a long put option. The only difference is the 'reverse logic' associated with put options. In other words, to make money on a FT-SE 100 index option, the market should fall.

Long put strategy

A long put strategy involves the purchase of a put option. It is a purely speculative strategy that has finite risk and unlimited reward (ie. it is a finite risk strategy).

Once again, let's scrutinise the profit/loss graph and try to understand what is really happening. When you first buy the put option, you establish the position for a net debit (since it cost you money), therefore you start off in negative territory. As the level of the index decreases, your put option becomes worth more and more as its intrinsic value increases. Again, we will want an option with a fairly high delta so that the price of the option increases at a good rate as the value of the index decreases. As the level of the index decreases further, so does the value of the put option until, at the break-even point, the gain in the value of the option exactly offsets the debit at which the position was established. The break-even point is very important to the option point because after this level, as the index goes lower, the long put option position will start to make a profit.

Let's now look at how we can tilt the probabilities in our favour as much as possible. The steps to be taken are listed below:

1. *Ideally, the chart of the FT-SE 100 index should be as bearish as possible. Things to look for in the chart include:*

appearance of a reversal pattern like a head and shoulders, double top, a dark cloud candlestick formation, downward break out of a symmetrical triangle etc. – all accompanied by good volume. Confirmation by stochastic indicators, moving averages, RSI etc.

2. *See if you can find any fundamental information to back your technical view (ie. bearish news – for the FT-SE 100 index, you may look at the general economy and views on interest rates) – if there is bearish news, then this further increases the probability of your long put position being profitable.*

3. *Establish support and resistance levels on the chart.*

4. *Preferably, the FT-SE 100 index should be bouncing off the resistance level on good volume.*

5. *Buy puts at a strike price above the resistance level. By doing so, you dramatically increase the probability of your put expiring in-the-money. You must decide over what period the index is likely to fall (ie. the likely speed of the fall) and buy put options whose life span will be longer than the expected time over which the move will occur. By doing this, you 'buy yourself more time' in case the index doesn't fall as quickly as you had anticipated, therefore decreasing the probability of your option expiring worthless.*

6. *Calculate your break-even point and determine how likely it is for the level of the FT-SE 100 index to decrease past the break-even level. The Option Evaluator™ can help you calculate this probability (the break-even probability). Generally, a probability over 45% can be considered favourable.*

7. *Make sure you are not paying 'over the odds'. In other words, make sure that the option is not overpriced; ie. make sure the percentage deviation from the theoretical value is not more than 7% (this is more a rule of thumb than anything else). It is not necessarily wrong to buy 'expensive' or sell 'cheap'. You must also take into consideration the current market environment/ sentiment.*

8. *Establish a **stop-loss** (normally set at slightly above the resistance level). Once this has been breached, ie. once the index closes above this level on heavy volume, the market is telling you that you are wrong. You must then **immediately** liquidate your long put position by selling the previously bought option. This will enable you to quickly close out of a position that has 'turned against you' – thereby, minimising your potential loss, ie. cutting your losses. The stop-loss must be established before the long put option position is established.*

9. *Establish a target level (using technical analysis or whatever form of analysis is available to you). This is the price which you expect the index to fall to (within your investment time horizon).*

10. *Once your established target level has been reached, ie. once the index closes at or below that level, take your profits by selling the puts you had previously bought. Although there are more sophisticated 'follow up' strategies, this is by far the simplest strategy available to novice option traders. In addition, it yields the most consistent results.*

Effect of timing

Once again, the position can be fine tuned to suit your aggressiveness or risk profile, by buying out-the-money puts if extremely bearish (ie. expecting a sudden drop in the value of the index in the short term), or slightly in-the-money puts if you are less aggressive. All that was said for the long call options regarding timing applies equally with the long put position.

* * *

Chapter 7
SOME MORE ADVENTUROUS OPTION STRATEGIES

Further trading strategies

In this chapter, we will look at slightly more adventurous option strategies (remaining within the finite risk domain). We shall look at strategies which 'combine' two options to form one combined position. These kind of strategies are often simply called spread trades.

Spread trades

There are several types of spread trade but I'll begin with a detailed analysis of one of the simpler types of spread, in particular, a calendar spread (also known as a time spread). But before we begin, it may be worthwhile to give the definition of a spread.

Spread trades (as applied to the options markets) are strategies in which the risk of one option position (known as a leg) is offset, at least to a certain degree, by another option position. In other words, one option benefits from an increase in the underlying and the other loses. Spread strategies typically involve offsetting positions in options with different exercise prices and/or different maturities (expiry dates).

Spreads can be broadly described under four categories:

1. *Calendar spreads.*

2. *Spreads based on differences in exercise prices (ie. vertical spreads).*

3. *Volatility spreads (ie. straddles and strangles).*

4. *Diagonal spreads.*

Calendar spread

The calendar spread in its simplest form is essentially an option strategy which implements a pair of options of the same type (both calls or puts). In addition, both options implemented in the strategy must meet the following criteria:

1. *Same underlying.*

2. *Same strike or exercise price.*

3. *The options must have different maturity or expiry dates.*

4. *The simultaneous sale of one option and the purchase of another, longer dated option.*

Given the above definition and criteria for a calendar spread, it would be easy to see that the following are all examples of calendar spreads:

1. *The sale of Euro-FTSE January 3675 calls along with the purchase of February 3675 calls .*

2. *The sale of May 3780 FT-SE 100 index calls along with the purchase of July 3780 FT-SE 100 index calls.*

In the broad definition of the term, a calendar spread is a horizontal spread (ie. neutral). The fact that both options implemented in the calendar spread have the same exercise price underpins the neutral philosophy of the calendar spread strategy. Before we look at the mechanics of a calendar spread more closely, it may well be appropriate to answer an important question that may be gnawing at your mind at this stage. Under what market conditions would a calendar spread be appropriate?

The horizontal nature of the calendar spread implies a 'net neutral view' of the underlying market. The term 'net neutral view' refers to the fact that the option investor expects the underlying instrument to remain relatively unchanged, ie. around the level of the exercise price of the spread by expiry of the near-dated option and, thereafter, to move in such a way that would result in a profit to the purchased option (the long leg of the spread). Expressed another way, the option investor expects the underlying instrument to move in a way that will erode the value of the written option at a faster rate than it will the purchased (far-dated) option. Under these conditions, the spread will widen and a profit may be earned at expiry of the written (shorter-dated) option.

Utilising call options, it is possible for an option investor to construct a more aggressive, bullish, calendar spread. Note that, even though such a strategy may be considered bullish, it is not as blatantly bullish as a long call position. This is because by establishing a calendar spread position, an investor is implying a 'cautiously bullish' stance. Why cautiously bullish? Well, because though the investor is bullish in the longer term (hence the purchased *far* dated option), he/she expects the underlying to remain below the strike price of the short or sold option (remember you generally sell options, then you are convinced that there is little chance of being assigned). Therefore, the view of an investor implementing a 'bullish' calendar spread is that the underlying will remain below the strike price of the written option (up to and until expiry) and after expriry of the sold (written) option, the underlying will rise above the strike price of the bought option, thus making a profit. Needless to say, a bearish calendar spread can also be established using put options with the same exercise price and different maturities.

An investor will normally implement a calendar spread if he/she envisages a degree of movement in the underlying after an initial period of 'relative inactivity'. The phrase 'relative inactivity' is used to emphasise the fact that the investor does not necessarily have to hold the view that the underlying will not move at all. If the investor holds such a view of total inactivity, then a more profitable strategy could be either a short straddle or a short strangle over a tight trading range. Another way of explaining the term relative inactivity would be (for a bullish calendar spread) the belief that the underlying will remain below a certain level (the strike price) during the life span of the sold call option, and for a bearish calendar spread, the belief that the underlying will remain above a certain level (the strike price) during the life span of the sold put option.

Although the concept of the calendar spread is essentially quite simple, it can be incorporated into more complicated strategies where a short-dated short position is established simultaneously with a longer-dated long position. For example, a more advanced option investor can implement straddles into a calendar strategy by selling a short-dated straddle and simultaneously buying a longer-dated straddle at the same strike. The following example may illustrate a typical scenario under which a 'bullish' calendar spread may be considered appropriate.

Suppose the FT-SE 100 index, after trending strongly upward for a length of time, starts trending sideways in a clearly defined range. Further assume that the FT-SE 100 index has previously attempted (unsuccessfully) to penetrate the resistance level in the past. We will now assume that there is some positive news or other fundamental data (economic reports), for example, low inflation and a possible rate cut due in a few months' time. A possible profitable strategy given the above scenario would be to establish a calendar spread by implementing slightly out-the-money calls. For such an 'aggressively bullish' calendar spread as described above, it is quite important that the FT-SE 100 index appears to be straining upward but needs some bullish news or development over time, to help it penetrate through its resistance level.

The main points to note in constructing such an 'aggressively bullish' calendar spread can be summarised in five succinct steps:

1. *Establish a resistance level that has been tested in the past.*

2. *Sell short dated calls at a strike price slightly higher than the resistance level.*

3. *There must be some fundamental or other news which is likely to make the share price penetrate the resistance level described in 1.*

4. Determine when the rally is likely to occur.

5. Buy call options at the same strike as the sold calls but with a longer maturity date (expiring after the expected bullish development).

A 'bullish' calendar spread is one in which the long position benefits from a rise in the value of the underlying, or, put more simply, a 'bullish' calendar spread is implemented when the investor is of the opinion that the underlying share will rise after a period of relative inactivity.

Unsurprisingly, the logic for implementing a 'bearish' calendar spread is almost the complete reverse for that of the 'bullish' calendar spread in that a support level is sought instead of a resistance level and the share must be generally trending sideways after a general downtrend and would have bounced off resistance several times.

We'll now turn our attention to vertical spreads.

Vertical spreads

A vertical spread is also a finite risk strategy and involves two options of the same class (ie. both calls or both puts) and the same expiry date but different strike prices. It also involves the sale of one option against the purchase of the other, thereby simultaneously establishing a short and a long in the combined position. There are basically two types of vertical spread:

1. Bull spreads.

2. Bear spreads.

A vertical spread is so named because of the shape of its profit graph. A look at the profit/loss graph on page 140 will illustrate this. The familiar shape of vertical spreads is caused by the 'vertical' difference in strike prices of the constituent options.

In general, a vertical spread must satisfy the following criteria:

1. *Both options involved in the spread must be of the same type, ie. both calls or puts.*

2. *Both options must have the same maturity (ie. expire on the same date).*

3. *The options must have different strike prices.*

4. *A lower strike option must be purchased along with the simultaneous sale of a higher strike option.*

From these criteria, it can be seen that this type of spread is very similar to the calendar spread discussed earlier. The main differences are that a calendar spread must have different expiry dates for the two options used in the spread and they must both have the same exercise price.

There are two types of vertical spread, bull spreads and bear spreads – the names reflecting whether the strategy benefits (ie. profits) from an increase or decrease in the price of the underlying. Both vertical spreads can be established by either calls or puts. Before we look further into how vertical spreads are implemented, we must first investigate the scenarios under which such strategies would appear attractive (relative to alternative strategies) to the option investor or, in other words, the scenarios under which the probability of a profit is greatly increased in favour of the option investor.

Vertical bull call spreads

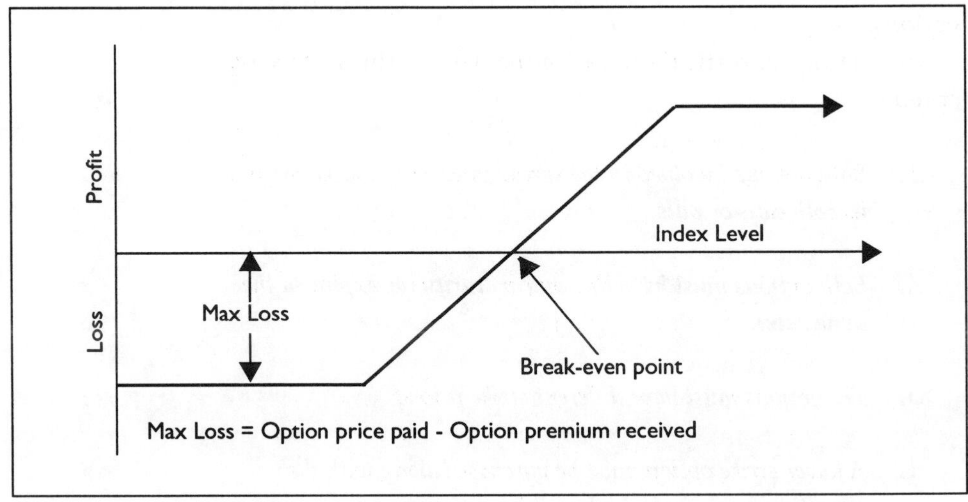

Figure 3.

This strategy is implemented by buying a call option with a lower strike price and simultaneously selling a call option with a higher exercise price. Both options should have the **same expiry date**. This strategy is less bullish than a straightforward long call strategy, and can be implemented if you expect a *slight* rise in the underlying share price. An additional advantage of this strategy is that the break-even is lower than that for a long call strategy. What this means is that you are more likely to make a profit (albeit a smaller one).

Assume that your view of the market is that it is likely to rise but not dramatically, ie. you are not overly bullish. In this scenario (assuming your view of the market is correct), a vertical bull spread is likely to be the most appropriate strategy to employ as it can be established at a lower initial price than, say, buying a call outright. The resulting spread will also outperform a simple call purchase up and until the time that the level of the FT-SE 100 index exceeds the higher exercise price of the sold option. The superiority in returns over a simple call purchase is due to the higher leverage available from the smaller initial outlay.

First of all, let me show you how this rather strange looking 'vertical step' profit/loss graph is achieved. By understanding how the profit/loss graph is constructed for a vertical bull call spread, you will be able to construct profit/loss graphs for your own positions. From these you can determine the break-even points and you can also see if the risk/reward offered by the strategy suits your risk profile. The table below makes the following assumptions: the current level of the FT-SE 100 index is 3700 and we want to establish a vertical bull call spread by simultaneously buying a 3650 FT-SE 100 index call and selling a 3800 FT-SE 100 index call for 75p and 25p respectively. From our earlier discussion, you may notice that this a fairly aggressive strategy, which requires the FT-SE 100 index to be above the 3800 level by expiry, in order to achieve maximum profit. The indicated call profits (+) or losses (-) are those that would be realised if the calls were liquidated at parity at expiry.

Index level at Expiry	3500	3550	3600	3650	3700	3750	3800	3850	3900
3650 call profit	-75	-75	-75	-75	-25	+25	+75	+125	+175
3800 call profit	+25	+25	+25	+25	+25	+25	+25	-25	-75
Total Profit	**-50**	**-50**	**-50**	**-50**	**0**	**+50**	**+100**	**+100**	**+100**

From the above table, a few points can be spotted:

- A vertical bull call spread is always established at a debit (this because the lower strike option is always more expensive than the sold higher strike call option).

- Maximum profit will be realised if the index is anywhere above the higher strike option.

- The initial debit is the maximum (and therefore known) loss possible for the position.

- The maximum loss will be incurred if the index is anywhere below the lower strike option.

- The break even point is given by the lower strike price plus the initial debit (in this case 3650 + 50).

It is well worth noting that this strategy has a reward/risk ratio of 2:1. In other words, if the FT-SE 100 index does move up to or above the 3800 level at expiry, a 100% return or profit will be realised over the holding period.

We shall now investigate how the vertical bull call spread actually establishes a profit. From the four criteria listed earlier, a vertical bull call spread is established by the simultaneous purchase of a call option at a particular strike, and the sale of another call at a higher strike. Normally, the lower strike option is in-the-money (and the higher strike option is slightly out-the-money). The lower strike option, being in-the-money, will have a higher delta (typically greater than 0.5) than the higher strike option and will therefore track the underlying asset more closely. What this means is that as the level of the index increases, the lower strike option increases in value more rapidly than the higher strike option. As the price of the index increases, however, the delta of the higher strike starts to accelerate and catch up with the delta of the lower strike option (remember the delta is a non-linear function of the underlying's price). By the time the level of the index reaches the strike price of the sold option (higher strike) both options will be moving more or less with the same speed in the same direction as the FT-SE 100 index (ie. becoming more profitable as the level of the index increases). It is at this point that the profit is capped. As both options increase in value at the same rate, gains made in the long (bought) option will be exactly offset by losses in the short (sold) option. The maximum profit (P) for a given vertical spread is the difference between the high (H) and low (L) strikes minus the initial debit (D). Expressed mathematically this is:

$$P = (H - L) - D$$

The maximum loss on a vertical bull call spread is the initial debit required to establish the position. Once again, vertical bull spreads can be ranked in terms of aggressiveness. The more aggressive spreads have a smaller probability of being profitable but promise much larger gains, whereas defensive spreads have a larger probability of becoming profitable though the returns are much lower. So what is an aggressive vertical bull call spread? An aggressive vertical bull call spread is simply a vertical bull call spread that incorporates options that are progressively out-the-money. Put more simply, the more out-the-money both options are, the more aggressive is the spread. Likewise, the more in-the-money both options are, the more defensive (ie. less aggressive) is the vertical bull spread strategy.

Vertical bull call spreads will outperform the outright purchase of call options (ie. long call positions) – as long as the index does not rise several points above the higher exercise price of the sold call option implemented in the vertical bull call spread.

Vertical bull put spreads

A vertical bull spread can also be implemented using puts instead of calls. This type of vertical bull spread is known as a

▲

vertical bull **put** spread and like the bull spread involving calls, it requires the simultaneous purchase of a lower strike option and the sale of a higher strike option. However, because puts are used instead of calls, the position is established at a credit. Apart from this basic difference the vertical bull put spread is very similar to the vertical bull call spread.

The following formulae allow us to calculate the details of a vertical bull put spread:

- Maximum profit = net credit received.

- Break-even point = higher exercise price – net credit received.

- Maximum risk = (higher strike price – lower strike price) – net credit received.

Vertical bear put spreads

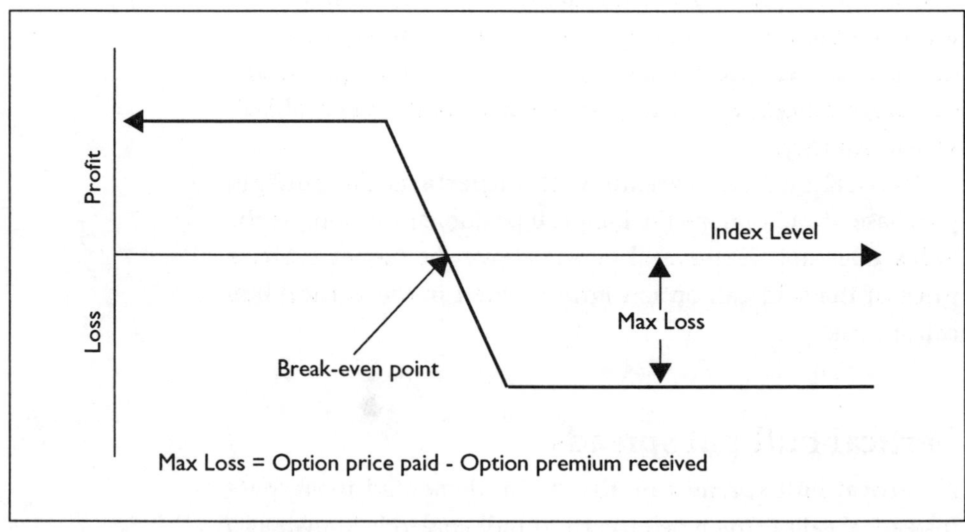

Figure 4.

As the 'bear' part of the name may suggest, this is a strategy that benefits (ie. becomes profitable) from a downward move, or a decrease in the level of the FT-SE 100 index (when using FT-SE 100 index options). This strategy is implemented by buying a put option with a higher strike price and simultaneously selling a put option with a lower exercise price. Both options must have the **same expiry date**. This strategy is less bearish than a straightforward long put strategy, and can be implemented if you expect a *slight* decline in the underlying share price. An additional advantage of this strategy is that the break-even is lower than that for a long put strategy. What this means is that you are more likely to make a (albeit smaller) profit.

Most of what has been said for bull spreads applies for bear spreads as well. That is, if you are not sure of a rapid downward movement in the FT-SE 100 index, but feel that the index is likely to experience a mild downward correction, then a vertical bear spread offers a much better return than an outright put purchase (long put positions).

The following numerical illustration of a vertical bear put spread will further illustrate this particular strategy.

Let's assume that the current level of the FT-SE 100 index is 3700 and that we have formed an opinion that the current level of the index is unsustainable and we would like to profit from the possible minor downward correction. Since we are not outrightly bearish on the market, a possibly profitable strategy would be a vertical bear put spread. We can establish such a spread by simultaneously buying a 3750 FT-SE 100 index put and selling a 3650 FT-SE 100 index put for 65p and 5p respectively. From our earlier discussion, you may notice that this a fairly defensive strategy; since it does not require the FT-SE 100 index to drop by much from its current level of 3700 to establish the maximum profit, we have also used an in-the-money put – further confirming that we are not aggressively bearish. The indicated call profits (+) or losses (-) are those that would be realised if the calls were liquidated at parity at expiry.

Index level at Expiry	3500	3550	3600	3650	3700	3750	3800	3850	3900
3750 put profit	+185	+135	+85	+35	-15	-65	-65	-65	-65
3650 put profit	-145	-95	-45	+5	+5	+5	+5	+5	+5
Total profit	**+40**	**+40**	**+40**	**+40**	**-10**	**-60**	**-60**	**-60**	**-60**

From the above table, a few points can be spotted:

- A vertical bear put spread is always established at a debit (this because the lower strike option is always more expensive than the sold higher strike call option).

- Maximum profit will be realised if the index is anywhere below the lower strike option.

- The initial debit is the maximum (and therefore known) loss possible for the position.

- The maximum loss will be incurred if the index is anywhere above the higher strike option.

- The break-even point is given by the higher strike price minus the initial debit (in this case 3750 – 50).

It is well worth noting that this strategy is particularly defensive and does not even require the level of the index to fall by much from its current level of 3700. In fact, the break-even point for this strategy is 3700! This is a very defensive strategy and the only chance of making a loss using this strategy arises when your initial analysis or view of the market is proved wrong by the market, ie. when the market moves up instead of down as you had anticipated (or the fall in the index is much more gradual than you had anticipated). You will not be surprised that such a defensive strategy has a rather low reward/risk ratio of 40/60 or 2:3 so, if the FT-SE 100 behaves as you had predicted and dips below the 3700 level (or is even at the current level of 3700) at expiry, a 66.7% return or profit will be realised over the holding period.

From the earlier definition, a vertical bear put spread is established by the simultaneous purchase of a put option at a particular strike, and the sale of another put at a lower strike. Normally, the lower strike option is out-the-money (and the higher strike option is slightly in-the-money). The higher strike put option being in-the-money will have a higher delta (typically greater than -0.5) than the higher strike option and will therefore track the underlying asset more closely. What this means is that as the level of the index decreases, the higher strike put option increases in value more rapidly than the lower strike option. As the level of the index continues to decrease, however, the delta of the lower strike put option starts to accelerate and catch up with the delta of the higher strike option (remember the delta is a non-linear function of the underlying's price). By the time the index level reaches the strike price of the sold option (lower strike) both options will be moving more or less with the same speed in the opposite direction of the FT-SE 100 index (remember that the value of a put always moves in the opposite direction to the value of the underlying, making the puts more profitable as the level of the index decreases). Because both options increase in value at the same rate, gains made in the long (bought) option will be exactly offset by losses in the short (sold) option. The maximum profit (P) for a given vertical spread is the difference between the high (H) and low (L) strikes minus the initial debit (D). Expressed mathematically this gives us:

$$P = (H - L) - D$$

The maximum loss on a vertical bear put spread is the initial debit required to establish the position. Once again, vertical bear spreads can be ranked in terms of aggressiveness. The more aggressive spreads have a smaller probability of being profitable but promise much larger gains whereas defensive spreads have a larger probability of becoming profitable though the returns are much lower. So what is an aggressive vertical bear put spread? An aggressive bear put spread is simply a vertical bear spread that incorporates put options that are progressively out-the-money. Put more simply, the more out-the-money both options are, the more aggressive is the spread. Likewise, the more in-the-money both options are, the more defensive (ie. less aggressive) is the vertical bear put spread strategy.

Vertical bear put spreads will outperform the outright purchase of put options (ie. long put positions) – as long as the index does not fall several points below the lower exercise price of the sold put option implemented in the vertical bear put spread.

The following formulae allow us to calculate the details of a vertical bear put spread:

- Maximum profit = (higher strike price – lower strike price) – initial debit.

- Break-even point = higher striking point – initial debit.

- Maximum risk = initial debit.

An example of a vertical bull put spread using FT-SE 100 index put options will be the simultaneous sale of the 3800 FT-SE 100 index put options, along with the purchase of the 3700 FT-SE 100 index put options (both having the same expiry date, of course).

A vertical bear spread can also be established using call

options. It also involves the sale of the lower strike option and the purchase of a higher strike option and profits accrue as the level of the index falls. This position is a credit spread, ie. it is established for a credit. This makes sense because if you think about it, a higher strike call option will always be cheaper than a lower strike call option.

Vertical bear call spreads

A vertical bear spread can also be implemented using calls instead of puts. This type of vertical bear spread is known as a vertical bear call spread and like the bear spread involving puts, it involves the simultaneous purchase of a higher strike option and the sale of a lower strike option. However, because calls are used instead of puts, the position is established at a credit. Apart from this basic difference the vertical bear call spread is very similar to the vertical bear put spread.

The following formulae allow us to calculate the details of a vertical bear call spread:

- Maximum profit = net credit received.

- Break-even point = lower exercise price + net credit received.

- Maximum risk = (higher strike price – lower strike price) – net credit received.

Volatility spreads

We will now look at some other forms of spread known as volatility spreads. They are known as volatility spreads because they involve the purchase (or sale) of a put and call, and the profitability of the position is independent of the direction of the movement of the index. That is, the position may make money if the index moves up or down by a sufficient amount, or if the index stays within a forecast 'band' during the life of the spread (how the volatility spread actually makes money depends on how the spread was established). Another way of explaining this kind of spread is that the profitability of the overall position is determined by the volatility (not direction of movement) of the underlying. As you may remember, at the beginning of Chapter One, I said that options allowed the investor to turn movements (or lack of them) in the markets into 'cash in the bank'. You do not have to be concerned about the direction of the market (ie. whether it is going to move upwards or downwards) when you are going to implement a volatility spread strategy. Your prime concern is the magnitude of a possible move, and the speed at which it is likely to occur. There are two main kinds of volatility spread. They are:

- Straddles.

- Strangles.

Long straddle strategy

A straddle is a combined position involving a put and a call option. The call and put must both have the **same exercise price** and **expiry date**. A long straddle can therefore be established by the simultaneous purchase of a call and put option with the same exercise price and the same expiry date. Such a strategy will be implemented if a strong increase in volatility is expected over the life span of the position, ie. the index will be expected either to soar by a large amount or dip (by an equally large amount) at expiry of the options implemented in the straddle. The investor who implements a long straddle is not interested in the direction of the movement of the underlying index, but is of the opinion that a large movement will occur in the underlying index. For this reason (the investor being interested solely in an increase in the volatility of the underlying), buying a straddle is known as buying volatility. Since a long straddle position can make a profit regardless of whether the index moves up or down (provided that the movement is large enough), this strategy has two break-even points. The following numerical example will further explain the concept of the straddle.

Suppose the current level of the FT-SE 100 index is 3700 and you expect a sharp movement in one direction or the other (as stated earlier, an option trader who embarks on a straddle strategy is not concerned in the direction of the impending movement, but rather on the magnitude or size of the anticipated movement). You may decide to purchase the 3700 FT-SE 100 index call and put options for 30 and 18 index points respectively. The straddle can be established for a total debit of 48 index points. Any movement of more than 48 points by the index will then result in the position becoming profitable.

Volatility spreads are slightly different from the previously described spreads since they do not care about the direction of the movement and are therefore neither bullish nor bearish. These spreads have two break-even points, the higher break-even point for the 'upside' move and the lower break-even point for the 'downside' move. The break-even points can be calculated as follows:

Lower break-even point = strike price – initial debit.

Higher break-even point = strike price + initial debit.

Therefore, the break-even points for the example given above are 3632 and 3748. This strategy will therefore realise a profit if the index moves by more than 48 points in either direction.

The profit/loss diagram below illustrates this.

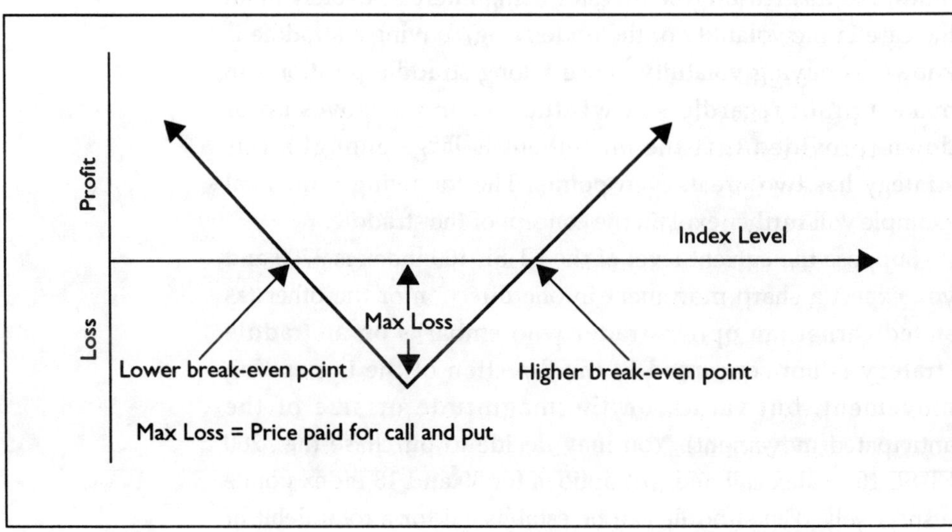

Figure 5.

Long strangle strategy

Like a straddle, a strangle is a combined position involving a put and a call option. However, the main difference is that the call and put must have **different exercise prices** but **the same expiry date**. Such a strategy will be implemented if the investor's view is that the index is unlikely to be 'within a predetermined band' at expiry of the options implemented in the strangle. In other words, the investor's view is that the FT-SE 100 is either going to be **above** level X by expiry, or **below** level Y by expiry. The investor who implements a long straddle is again not interested in the direction of the movement of the underlying index, but is of the opinion that a large movement will occur in the underlying index. For this reason (the investor

▲

being interested solely in an increase in the volatility of the underlying), buying a strangle is known as buying volatility. Since a long strangle position can make a profit regardless of whether the index moves up or down (provided that the movement is large enough), this strategy has two break-even points. The following numerical example will further explain the concept of the strangle.

Suppose that the current level of the FT-SE 100 index is 3700 and that you expect a sharp movement in one direction or the other. You may decide to purchase the 3700 FT-SE 100 index call options for 30 index points, and the 3650 FT-SE 100 index put options for 5 index points respectively. So the straddle can be established for a total debit of 35 index points. You may have noticed another slight difference between the strangle and the straddle – the strangle is normally considerably cheaper than a straddle established at either of its strike prices. In the particular example given above, any movement of more than 35 points by the index (from either strike) will result in the position becoming profitable.

A strangle also has two break-even points, the higher break-even point for the 'upside' move and the lower break-even point for the 'downside' move. The break-even points can be calculated as follows:

Lower break-even point = put strike price – initial debit.

Higher break-even point = call strike price + initial debit.

Therefore, the break-even points for the example given above are 3632 and 3736. This strategy will therefore realise a profit if the index moves by more than 48 points in either direction. The profit/loss diagram on the next page illustrates this.

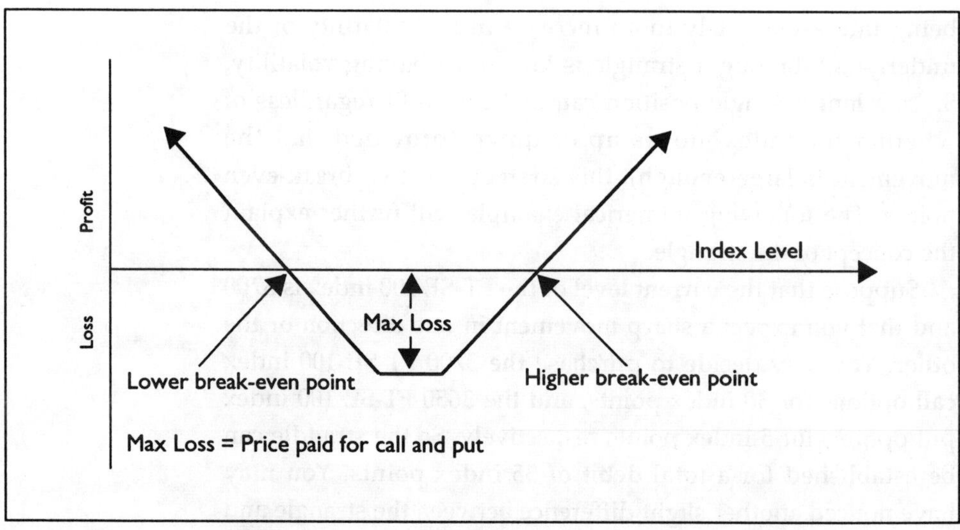

Figure 6.

In all the examples of spreads given previously, it is important to check the level of option premium available when writing options. The more expensive an option is, the more profitable any spread strategy which involves selling the expensive option will be. Sometimes the level of premiums available may make a particular spread strategy more attractive than another. For example, a vertical bull put spread may appear more attractive than a vertical bull call spread strategy, or a straddle may appear more attractive than a strangle. The break-even points (which are determined by the exercise prices and the option premiums), along with your analysis and view of the underlying market, should help you to choose 'attractive' strategies that should help tilt the odds in your favour.

* * *

Chapter 8
USING AN OPTIONS BROKER

Finding a broker

After learning all about the different types of option, their various sensitivities (the greeks) and looking at a few option strategies, you are now well equipped with the 'theory' of options. You may now want to put your knowledge into practice and actually start trading index options. However, there are a few things that need to be mentioned before you start trading options.

In this chapter we will discuss what to look for in a broker as a novice option investor (or indeed as a sophisticated option investor). A broker can provide a lifeline to an option trader as the broker is in direct contact with the market and will be aware of relevant news as it occurs. One way in which a broker can also help an option investor is by relaying news from the trading floor (though, admittedly, this is most useful to day traders, which, by definition, excludes most private investors).

The first step to take in trading options is to get yourself a broker. A list of such brokers is available from LIFFE (0171 623 0444). To trade options you must select a stockbroker (if you don't already have one) and open a trading account. You will have to sign and return a derivatives risk warning before you can start trading options. It is especially important as a novice option investor that you make it quite clear to your broker that you are a beginner and that you may require some 'hand holding' at times. It may also be advisable to agree to paper trade for a mutually agreeable period before commencing 'proper trading'. Having said that, it is important that you realise your broker only earns commissions on *actual trades* that you make and is therefore not very likely to recommend long periods of paper trading. It is for you and your broker to decide what constitutes a reasonable length of time for paper trading.

It is important that your broker is willing to help you out even during your non-commission generating paper trading period. If you sense some hesitation from the broker regarding paper trading, then it is most likely that you are better off with another broker who will be willing to provide some 'hand holding' during your paper trading days and during your first few trades. It is amazing the effect that the first few trades have on an investor's confidence. It is probably a case of 'first impressions last' being carried too far.

Having started paper trading, you must also bear in mind that it is vital not to use terminology that you do not fully understand just to impress, as, at the best of times, this will cause confusion and annoyance and in the worst case could actually result in an order different from the one you had originally intended being carried out on your behalf. When you actually start trading, it is important to remember that it is *your* money that is being invested and under no circumstances should you allow yourself to be talked into establishing a position in which you do not feel comfortable, or do not fully understand.

We will now discuss the various order types that are available (an order is the instruction you give your broker to buy or sell an option on your behalf). It is very important, when trading options, to use the right terms as well as the right order, to explain to your broker the position that you wish to establish on completion of your trade. The following terms are used:

What you need to be aware of – types of order

- Opening Purchase: A trade whereby an option investor buys an option (becomes the holder).

- Opening Sale: A trade whereby an option investor sells an option (ie. writes an option). This trade is potentially dangerous to the unwary investor.

- Closing Purchase: A trade whereby an option investor who has previously written an option buys back an identical option, effectively extinguishing his/her obligation as a writer.

- Closing Sale: A trade whereby an option investor who has previously bought an option sells an identical option to the one previously bought, thereby effectively extinguishing his/her right as a holder.

It is extremely dangerous and inadvisable for novice investors to write options for the reasons explained previously. More advanced option investors may write options as part of a spread (see previous chapter), because the nature of the spread caps the maximum loss of the spread to a finite, known amount. Writing options without having sufficient cash to purchase back the options at the market price (in the case of index options) is known as *naked writing* or *running naked* and, as the name may suggest, can have particularly nasty consequences!

Here are a few more kinds of order that I have thrown in for good measure, which can be used to enhance your orders. They can make your orders less ambiguous – but make sure you understand them fully before attempting to use them when trading.

ORDER	MEANING
Market Order or 'At best'	This is an order to your broker to buy or sell an option at the best possible price as soon as the order gets to the exchange floor.
Limit Order	This is an order to buy or sell an option up to a specified price (the limit). Sometimes a limit order may specify a discretionary margin for the floor broker, e.g. 'buy 5 American Style June 3700 calls at 70 with a penny discretion'. The problem with limit orders is that they may not get 'filled', or actioned, if the option price does not reach the limit specified.
Stop Order	This type of order may be used to protect a profit or loss. It is in effect a special type of limit order. This order is treated as a market order when the stop price is reached and is therefore sometimes known as a market if touched order.

No one expects you to know or remember all these various kinds of order, so do not feel under pressure to learn them. You can always find other ways of making your orders precisely clear to your broker, although these are the well known terms used in the markets.

Margin requirements

Certain strategies which involve the writing of options (ie. opening sale transactions) require margin. When an option investor undertakes such a margined transaction, he is required to deposit cash or collateral to ensure that he is capable of meeting any future liabilities (his obligations as a writer) upon exercise or closing out of his position. Funds deposited for these purposes are held in a margin account. Every day, the exchange provides a set of data known as a risk array, which allows brokers to calculate margin requirements for their clients. If there is a shortfall in a customer's account either due to a sharp movement in the FT-SE 100 index or assignment, the client receives a *margin call* from the broker, and has to meet his/her obligation as a writer, to make further payments to 'top up' his/her margin account.

Paper trading

It is advisable for investors completely new to the market, to 'test the waters' before committing any money. Paper trading means going through the motions of trading without actually committing money to the market. This may involve getting quotes from your broker and/or placing 'pseudo orders'. If you do place 'pseudo orders' with your broker, it is important that you state clearly that they are not real orders, because several brokerage houses record all telephone conversations that take place between clients and brokers during the course of the day.

The way to go about paper trading successfully in FT-SE 100 index options is to carry out some initial research on your own, to decide what the market is likely to do – that is, by how much it is likely to move (if at all), in which direction, and within what time frame. Investors normally use fundamental/technical analysis in determining these parameters. Technical analysis may have a slight advangtage here though, because timing is crucially important in option investing.

Taking the plunge

A word of warning. Most investors make their first purchases from emotional or sentimental motives like: "I always do my shopping at XYZ Ltd so I might just as well get some shares in them", or "my mother-in-law works at ABC, so I don't care how well the company is doing, I'm simply not going to buy any shares in *her* company!". Investments must only be made in the cold light of rationality, following detailed analysis and research. Last but not least, do not enter into the markets for the sake of 'being in the market'. If you can't find anything interesting in the market, just sit tight and leave your money in a bank until something interesting crops up. It usually does, if you wait long enough. There is a well-known saying in the City of London : "If in doubt, get out!".

To be successful in any investment (options included), the three most important rules (in order of importance) are:

1. *Preservation of capital.*

2. *Striving to achieve consistency in returns.*

3. *Maximising returns when the probabilities are 'tilted in your favour' by taking on more aggressive trades.*

Rule number 1
As an investor, your foremost and primary concern should be the preservation of capital. It is easy to lose money in all types of investment if sufficient preparation is not made before the

investment is carried out.. One of the simpler ways of ensuring that your investment capital is preserved is by proper money management techniques. The simplest and most commonly known money management technique involves the establishment of stop-losses and profit targets as described earlier on in this book. It is important that you stick to these targets once they have been set.

Rule number 2

This is the investment equivalent of the popular adage 'a bird in the hand is worth two in the bush'. It is far more prudent (unless you are absolutely sure of the outcome of your investment), to implement less aggressive or even defensive strategies. As we saw in the earlier example given for the defensive vertical bear put spread, the index did not even have to decrease from its level of 3700 for a profit to be made. Even though the profit from that strategy would pale into insignificance when compared with the return possible from an aggressive out-the-money long put position, it is generally safer to stick with the defensive strategies since they have a greater probability of being profitable.

Rule number 3

After extensive analysis (which could include using the software accompanying this book), an investor can be fairly convinced that his/her view of the market has a high probability of being correct. In these cases when you are very sure that you are correct (and I'm not talking about gut feeling here), then the best thing to do would be to use a **proportion** of your portfolio (a percentage you can afford to lose without worrying) and then bet **heavily and aggressively** in accordance with your view. If your view is confirmed, you will realise a percentage gain on your initial stake that could run into four figures. It is important to remember that when speculating in this manner, you must use only that proportion of your portfolio that you can afford to lose, otherwise you will be in violation of Rule number 1 and you are not likely to remain in the market for very long.

Conclusion

* Options can be as complicated as you want them to be.

* Don't get involved in trades which you don't understand – keep things simple (at least initially).

* Don't get involved in trades which you don't feel comfortable with – ie. strategies not matched with your risk profile.

* Don't get involved in a position without fully evaluating the option and/or checking if there are better alternatives (ie. other series or strategies).

* Protect your profits by setting a target level for the index before implementing any strategy and EXIT your position once your target has been reached.

* Limit your losses by establishing a stop-loss level for the FT-SE 100 index before implementing any strategy and EXIT your position once your stop-loss is breached.

* Don't buy an option just because it appears 'cheap'.

Options are best used for portfolio enhancement – increasing the return available on your holding and reducing the volatility of the overall portfolio by hedging. When speculating, it is often advisable to speculate with only a percentage of your portfolio (the precise percentage figure being determined by your risk profile). Generally, option portfolios are not recommended to private investors since the volatility of returns would require a level of monitoring that may not be available to them. However, a private investor who is aware of the risks involved (and comfortable with them) may instruct his/her broker to construct and undertake the monitoring of such an option portfolio on his/her behalf.

If you restrict your option strategies to finite risk strategies, and think about the consequences of your actions **before** implementing your strategy, options provide an interesting way to turn *each and every possible movement* in shares, market indices, bonds, currencies and interest rates into cash in your bank account. The importance of finite risk option strategies is that you can sleep at night, knowing that in the worst case scenario, all you will lose is your initial premium or 'stake'. In the best case scenario, however, your profits could be unlimited! Option investors have been known to turn an initial 'stake' with a couple of hundreds of pounds into tens of thousands of pounds. Such phenomenal gearing (in addition to the choice of finite risk) exists only in the domain of options.

The **three golden rules** that an option investor must remember are:

- Keep it simple – don't get involved in option strategies you don't understand.

- Do not just throw money at options without thinking about what you're investing in – although speculative option trading has sometimes been compared to the lottery or betting, the success (or otherwise) of an option trade is not completely dependent on chance. By thinking before you act, you can significantly weigh the odds in your favour.

- If the market proves you wrong – get out (ie. close your position by selling on your 'bet' to someone else with a different view). You don't have to lose the full amount of your 'stake' to realise that you are wrong. Remember – the options market is no place for pride!

Good luck and happy investing!

* * *

GLOSSARY OF OPTION TERMINOLOGY

American Style A type of option which can be exercised on any trading day during the life of the option.

Assign When an option holder exercises his/her option, the counter-party (writer) is randomly selected by the exchange to fulfil his/her obligation to the holder. The writer is then said to have been assigned.

At-the-money An option whose exercise price is the same as the price of the underlying.

Bear An investor who has the view that share prices are going to fall.

Bull An investor who has the view that share prices are going to rise.

Call option An option that confers upon the owner the right to buy the underlying at a predetermined price (the exercise price) at some point in the future.

CBOT Chicago Board Of Trade – the world's largest options exchange, and also the first such exchange to be established.

Delta This is the change in an options price, given a one point change in the price of the underlying.

Derivative A financial asset whose value is derived from the value of another underlying instrument.

European Style A type of option which can only be exercised on its day of expiry.

Exercise This term refers to when an option holder exercises his/her option.

Exercise Price The price at which an option holder can exercise his/her option.

Expire An option is said to expire when it comes to the end of its life.

Expiry Date The date beyond which a particular option series ceases to exist.

Finite Risk Strategy An option strategy in which the maximum loss is quantifiable and known from the onset of the position – examples include buying options, and certain 'spread' strategies – see section on Option Strategies.

Giver An option buyer.

Hedging A strategy whereby an investor 'insures' a holding against future adverse movements of the market.

In-the-money An option that has intrinsic value.

Intrinsic Value This is the (positive) difference between the price of the underlying and the exercise price of the option.

LIFFE (London International Financial Futures and Options Exchange) – the main UK exchange for trading in options.

Long (position) This is a market position that tends to benefit when shares goes up and tends to suffer when shares fall in price. An example of such a position is buying a call option.

Margin This is the amount of capital required by the exchange to cover for short positions.

Market Maker A market participant who takes on an obligation to make a market in a particular share by offering to buy and sell the shares on his/her own account – acting as principal.

Naked Writing An option strategy which involves selling an option without owning the underlying. This is a potentially dangerous strategy for inexperienced option investors as it involves finite reward and unlimited risk.

Option Class All options of the same type (ie. call or put) based on the same underlying share. Calls and puts belong to different classes.

Option Series	All options of the same class (see previous page) and with the same exercise price and expiry date.
Out-the-money	A call option whose exercise price exceeds the price of the underlying share, or a put option whose excercise price is below the price of the underlying share.
Position	A trade. Selling something you do not own is known as 'shorting' or a short position, and buying something is known as establishing a long position.
Premium	The market price of the option.
Put Option	An option that confers upon the owner the right to sell the underlying shares at a predetermined price (the exercise price) at some point in the future.
Short (position)	This is a market position that tends to benefit when share prices fall and tends to suffer when share prices rise. An example of such a position is writing (selling) a call option.
Speculation	Normally an investment that has a relatively short life span which is undertaken on a strong belief that a particular share (or the whole market) will behave in a particular fashion over the time the investment is held.
Strike or Exercise	The price at which an option holder can exercise the right to sell/buy the underlying share.
Taker	An option writer
Time Value	The difference between an options premium and its intrinsic value.

Transaction Costs Costs incurred in establishing a position, ie. brokerage charges etc.

Underlying This is the financial asset from which an option's value is determined. For the purpose of this book, the underlying is always the FT-SE 100 index unless explicitly specified otherwise.

Volatility A measure of the degree at which the price of the underlying tends to fluctuate – the higher the volatility, the greater the potential for increased profit but the greater the risk of a loss. Volatility is of paramount importance when determining the price of an option.

Writer A writer is an option trade counter-party who takes on the obligation of selling the option to the buyer. Option writing can be a finite profit, unlimited loss strategy and must not be attempted by novice option investors.

* * *

The author can be contacted at:

Neil. Osborne @dial.pipex.com   Internet (e-mail)

Index

TRADED OPTIONS – A PRIVATE INVESTOR'S GUIDE:
How to invest more profitably
by Peter Temple
(1995: Price £16.95 Hardback)
ISBN 0 948935 06 4

This book is about making money by improving the returns you can achieve from the stockmarket. Although there may be risks involved, a clear understanding of how traded options work and a disciplined approach can reap substantial rewards.

Written by experienced author and financial journalist Peter Temple, this book explains traded options in a clear and methodical step-by-step style.

"Traded options are a powerful tool in the hands of a knowledgeable investor. This book will develop a comprehensive understanding of this fast moving and fascinating aspect of the stockmarket." David Charters, Managing Director, Investment Research of Cambridge Ltd.

TRADED OPTIONS – A PRIVATE INVESTOR'S GUIDE will help you to master the often daunting subject matter of options and enable you to add a vital new dimension to your stockmarket trading.

Rushmere Wynne

are publishers of finance, investment and management books
If you would like a copy of our current catalogue

Please write to:

Rushmere Wynne
4-5 Harmill
Grovebury Road
Leighton Buzzard
Bedfordshire
LU7 8FF

or fax: 01525 852037   or phone: 01525 853726